DEPARTMENT OF THE NAVY
HEADQUARTERS UNITED STATES MARINE CORPS
3000 MARINE CORPS PENTAGON
WASHINGTON, DC 20350-3000

I0427370

HH-46D/E (SAR) T&R MANUAL

DEPARTMENT OF THE NAVY
HEADQUARTERS UNITED STATES MARINE CORPS
3000 MARINE CORPS PENTAGON
WASHINGTON, DC 20350-3000

NAVMC 3500.21
C 4610
APR 24 2007

NAVMC 3500.21

From: Commandant of the Marine Corps
To: Distribution List

Subj: HH-46D/E (SAR) T&R MANUAL

Ref: (a) NAVMC DIR 3500.14

Encl: (1) HH-46D/E (SAR) T&R MANUAL

1. <u>Purpose</u>. To revise standards and regulations regarding the training of HH-46D/E (SAR) aircrew per the reference.

2. <u>Information</u>. This revision incorporates modified Plans of Instruction (POI) to facilitate the introduction of the CH-46E model aircraft that will eventually replace the CH-46D model. The Basic POI is for all aircrew who are converting to the CH-46D/E for the purpose of SAR and all Refresher pilots who have previously flown SAR in the CH-46D/E. A Series Conversion POI is provided for SAR qualified pilots current in the CH-46D who are converting to the CH-46E.

3. <u>Recommendations</u>. Recommended changes to this order are invited, and may be submitted via the syllabus sponsor and the appropriate chain of command to: **Commanding General, Training and Education Command, Aviation** Training Branch via e-mail (refer to http://www.tecom.usmc.mil/atb/contacts .htm) or the Defense Message System using the following plain language address: CG TECOM QUANTICO VA ATB.

4. <u>Reserve Applicability</u>. This manual is applicable to the Marine Corps Total Force.

5. <u>Certification</u>. Reviewed and approved this date.

GEORGE J. FLYNN
By direction

DISTRIBUTION: PCN 10033195700

    Copy to: 7000260 (2)
             8145001 (1)

DISTRIBUTION STATEMENT A: Approved for public release; distribution is unlimited.

CHAPTER 1

HH-46D/E (SAR) PILOT

FIGURES

* * **N O T E** * *

Aircrews shall include Crew Resource Management as part of their brief.

CHAPTER 1

HH-46D/E (SAR) PILOT

100. <u>MARINE SEARCH AND RESCUE UNIT - HH-46D/E</u>

1. <u>General</u>. The capabilities defined and described in the core capability and unit template sections are provided to ensure each like-SAR unit maintains a common base of training and depth of capabilities. When sources permit and when, in the judgment of the commander, additional training would significantly increase the unit's Search and Rescue capability, training to a level above these base capabilities is permitted. It is incumbent upon and expected of commanders to balance any increase in the depth of core capabilities against the long-term health and readiness of his unit while staying within resource constraints.

2. <u>Mission</u>. To provide heliborne SAR capabilities to tenant aviation units. Additional missions are secondary in nature and shall be accepted on a not-to-interfere basis only.

3. <u>Mission Essential Task List (METL)</u>

    a. Provide Search and Rescue for tenant aircraft.

    b. Provide supplemental Search and Rescue asset for U. S. Coast Guard and U.S. Air Force.

    c. Provide MEDEVAC capability to local civilian agencies as required, on a not-to-interfere basis.

    d. Provide airborne fire-fighting capability for MCAS facilities and to supplement local area Forest Service assets.

    e. Provide supplemental Search and Rescue to local civilian agencies for non-law enforcement type missions such as searches, fire fighting, disaster response, or civilian MEDEVAC, when civilian agencies cannot respond.

    f. Provide utility and logistical support missions for MCAS activities as directed by the Director of Operations, Marine Corps Installations (MCI) EAST.

    g. Enhance public relations for the Commanding General, MCI EAST through static displays and flight demonstrations as authorized by higher authority.

4. <u>Table of Organization</u>

> 3 HH-46D/E helicopters
> 8 Pilots
> 9 Crew Chiefs
> 6 SAR Swimmers
> 4 SAR Medical Technicians

5. <u>Squadron Core Capability</u>

    a. A core capable squadron is able to sustain the following minimum performance on a daily basis during sustained search and rescue operations, assuming at least 100% Primary Authorized Allowance (PAA), 90% in reporting status, and 90% T/O on hand in all MOSs. If <90%, core capability will be degraded by like-percentage. The extent to which a core capable squadron is able to surge beyond its core capability is situationally dependent.

b. A core capable squadron is able to launch 1 full mission capable aircraft crewed by fully qualified aircrew at all times. This aircraft must be airborne within 15 minutes of alert when operating under SAR Condition I and 1 hour under SAR Condition II.

6. <u>METL Core Skill Matrix</u>. Unit core skills directly support the unit METL as follows.

METL	CORE SKILL								CORE PLUS		
	OFT	FAM	INST	CAL	FF	SAR	NVG	NSAR	RAP	FCLP	CQ
a. Provide Search and Rescue for tenant aircraft.	X	X	X	X		X	X	X	X		
b. Provide supplemental Search and Rescue asset for U.S. Coast Guard and U.S. Air Force.	X	X	X	X		X	X	X			
c. Provide MEDEVAC capability to local civilian agencies as required, on a not-to-interfere basis.	X	X	X	X		X	X	X	X		
d. Provide airborne fire-fighting capability for MCAS facilities and to supplement local Forest Service assets.	X	X	X	X	X						
e. Provide supplemental Search and Rescue to local civilian agencies for non-law enforcement type missions such as searches, fire fighting, disaster response, or civilian MEDEVAC, when civilian agencies cannot respond.	X	X	X	X	X	X	X	X	X		
f. Provide utility and logistical support missions for MCAS activities as directed by the Director of Operations, Marine Corps Installations (MCI) EAST.	X	X	X	X	X	X	X	X	X	X	X
g. Enhance public relations for the Commanding General, MCI EAST through static displays and flight demonstrations as authorized by higher authority.	X	X	X	X		X					

Table title: HH-46 SAR   CORE SKILL TO METL MATRIX

101. PROGRAMS OF INSTRUCTION (POI)

1. All HH-46D/E SAR pilots are required to obtain the 7562 MOS and receive all Core Skills training in the FMF prior to undergoing Basic SAR training in either the HH-46D and/or HH-46E.

2. The Basic POI is for all CH-46E pilots who are making a conversion to the HH-46D/E for the purpose of SAR and all refresher pilots who have previously flown SAR in the HH-46D/E. The Basic POI includes all 200 - 400 events.

3. The Series Conversion POI is for SAR qualified pilots current in the HH-46D who are making a conversion to the HH-46E.

102. POI for BASIC SAR PILOT

WEEKS	COURSE/PHASE	ACTIVITY
56	Core Plus Training in CH-46E	FMF
1	SAR Ground Training	MCAS New River
9	Flight Training	VMR-1

103. POI FOR SERIES CONVERSION

WEEKS	COURSE/PHASE	ACTIVITY
56	Core Plus Training in CH-46E	FMF
1	SAR Ground Training	MCAS New River
4	Flight Training	VMR-1

104. POI FOR INSTRUCTOR UNDER TRAINING

WEEKS	COURSE/PHASE	ACTIVITY
3	Flight Training	VMR-1

105. SQUADRON LEVEL TRAINING

NATOPS Flight Manual and Pilot NATOPS Pocket Checklist
Instrument Procedures and Changes
Flight Safety
SAR Mission Planning and Briefing
SAR TACAID
Global Positioning System (GPS) Operation
Squadron and Air Station Standard Operating Procedures (SOPs)
Local Course Rules
Survival
Flight Training Movies

106. FLIGHT TRAINING FOR BASIC AND REFRESHER PILOTS. All initial syllabus flights shall be flown with a designated NATOPS Instructor or Assistant NATOPS Instructor. Assistant NATOPS and NATOPS Instructors are not required for FCLP and CQ events but shall be flown in accordance with OPNAVIST 3710.7.

107. FLIGHT TRAINING FOR SERIES CONVERSION

1. Core Skill Basic, NVG Core Skill Advanced, and Core Skill Plus qualifications per this Manual and the CH-46E T&R Manual remain current upon transfer to the HH-46D/E, pending approval of the SAR unit commanding officer.

2. All initial syllabus flights shall be flown with a designated NATOPS Instructor

108. REQUIREMENTS FOR SAR H2P DESIGNATION

1. Complete all seven SAR academic lectures.

2. Complete SAR Open Book Examination.

3. Current Instrument rating, current SAR H2P NATOPS Check and CRM Check in appropriate model aircraft.

4. SAR T&R codes complete through the 200 level syllabus (with exception of 254 and 260) and night SAR T&R codes 300, 323 and 324. (If the pilot is both NSQ and current in model, the night syllabus can be waived.) HH-46D/E H2Ps that have not completed the night SAR syllabus may be designated Day SAR H2P.

109. <u>REQUIREMENTS FOR SAR HAC DESIGNATION</u>

1. Meet the requirements for SAR H2P per paragraph 108.

2. SAR T&R codes complete through NSAR 340. A pilot may be designated Day SAR HAC at the discretion of the Commanding Officer once SAR T&R codes complete through SAR 260.

120. <u>GROUND/ACADEMIC TRAINING</u>

<u>COURSE</u>	<u>ACTIVITY</u>
SAR Ground School/SAR Pilot Training Course	VMR-1
HH-46E SAR Simulator	MCAS New River

130. <u>FLIGHT/SIMULATOR PERFORMANCE REQUIREMENTS</u>

1. <u>Purpose</u>. Become familiar with aircraft limitations and emergency procedures. Develop proficiency in SAR planning, in-flight procedures, and knowledge of safety regulations that pertain to SAR operations. Become familiar with SAR procedures and requirements.

2. <u>General</u>

    a. Pilots current in the model HH-46D helicopter will be programmed to fly the Series Conversion (SC) syllabus. All other pilots will be programmed to fly the complete program of instruction regardless of qualifications.

    b. All initial flights shall be flown with a designated NATOPS/Assistant NATOPS Instructor.

    c. Local commands are granted the authority to waive requirements that are not applicable to the local operating environment.

    d. All flights shall terminate with a comprehensive debrief with emphasis on aircrew performance using all evaluation techniques.

    e. Aircrews shall fly events annotated with an N at least 30 minutes after official sunset. Aircrews may fly events annotated with (N) at night.

    f. Aircrews shall fly events annotated with an NS with Night Vision Devices (NVDs) for the entire flight. Aircrews may fly events with (NS) with the option of using NVDs.

    g. Flight training events not flown in Core Skill Introduction training shall be flown in the subsequent stage of training.

    h. All flights annotated with an E shall be evaluated per T&R Program Manual.

    i. Environmental conditions (day or night) or Night Systems conditions shall be annotated in flight events and the syllabus matrix as follows:

Code	Requirement
D	Shall be flown or conducted during day.
N	Shall be flown or conducted at night (using available night vision devices or flown unaided).
(N)	May be flown or conducted day or night; if at night, available night vision devices may be used or flown unaided.
NS	Shall be flown or conducted at night using available night vision devices.
(NS)	May be flown or conducted day or night; if at night, available night vision devices shall be used.
N*	Event Shall be flown or conducted at night unaided.
(N*)	Event may be flown or conducted at night; if at night, shall be flown unaided.

3. <u>Altitudes</u>. All syllabus sorties should be flown at an altitude commensurate with the sortie description and safety of flight.

4. <u>Refly Interval</u>. Figure 1-1 shows refly interval and Mission Readiness Percentage (MRP) for MOS 7562.

5. <u>Aircrew Evaluation Flights</u>. All pilots are required to have an evaluation form filled out annually upon completion of the following:

    a. NATOPS Check (RQD-600, RQD-602, RQD-603, RQD-640).

    b. Instrument Check (RQD-601).

    c. Any flight in the Core Skill Advanced, Core Skill Basic, or Core Skill Advanced phase as recommended by the Squadron Standardization Board.

    d. Squadrons shall use Figure 1-2, the Aircrew Training Form for any evaluated flights.

6. <u>Crew Resource Management (CRM)</u>. Aircrews shall include CRM techniques as part of their brief.

131. <u>CORE SKILL BASIC TRAINING</u>

1. <u>Simulator Training</u>

    a. <u>Purpose</u>. Familiarize all pilots with HH-46 normal cockpit procedures, Crew Resource Management (CRM), systems operations and limitations, emergency procedures, and to introduce instrument flight and emergency procedures in a SAR environment.

    b. <u>General</u>. Initial simulator training shall be completed by all pilots prior to starting the flight syllabus. Simulator training will be conducted at an appropriate H-46 SAR simulator. Refresher training shall be conducted annually thereafter. CRM shall always be stressed.

c. Initial Simulator Training (3 Periods, 3.0 Hours)

OFT-200   1.0   SC,R   2F191

Goal. Normal procedures, start engage, shut-down and emergency procedures.

Requirement. Introduce system differences between HH-46 aircraft start engage, shut-down, and in-flight emergencies.

OFT-201   1.0   R   2F191

Goal. Doppler introduction.

Requirement. Discuss emergency water landing in a night environment single engine takeoff from water at night and emergency exits. Introduce low level instrument flight over water, Doppler pattern and procedures, and engine failures in the Doppler pattern. Review OFT-S200.

OFT-202   1.0   SC,R   2F191

Goal. Doppler and emergency procedures review.

Requirement. Review OFT-201.

2. Familiarization

    a. Purpose. Become familiar with aircraft flight characteristics, limitations, and emergency procedures; develop proficiency in all maneuvers contained in the familiarization stage.

    b. General

        (1) Prior to FAM-203, conduct a thorough preflight and postflight inspection with a qualified SAR pilot.

        (2) In preparing for a sortie, pilots shall study emergencies per the NATOPS Flight Manual. The pilot's pocket checklist lacks important information presented in the NATOPS Flight Manual. In addition to the emergency procedures, study the aircraft systems related to each particular malfunction.

    c. Crew Requirements. IP/PUI/CC.

    d. Flight Training (3 Flights, 4.5 Hours)

FAM-203   1.5   R   1 HH-46D/E

Goal. Conduct an area familiarization.

Requirement

    (1) Brief/Discuss. Differences between HH-46D/E and CH-46E aircraft.

    (2) Introduce

        (a) Normal cockpit, start, radio procedures, and taxiing.

        (b) Local course rules.

(c) All familiarization procedures as per NATOPS.

(d) Local hospital and landing area familiarization.

Performance Standard. Pilot shall be able to identify differences between HH-46D/E and CH-46E series helicopters, and perform familiarization maneuvers per NATOPS.

Prerequisite. Conduct through preflight and postflight with qualified SAR pilot.

EP-204   1.5   SC,R   1 HH-46E

Goal. Conduct emergency procedure familiarization.

Requirement

(1) Brief/Discuss. Differences between HH-46D/E and CH-46E aircraft.

(2) Introduce/Review

(a) All familiarization maneuvers with emphasis on hover and in-flight single engine emergencies.

(b) Perform practice autorotations and practice single engine flight.

(c) All emergency procedures/system failures.

Performance Standard. Pilot shall demonstrate knowledge of aircraft systems, perform basic FAM maneuvers, and be able to satisfactorily perform emergency procedures per NATOPS.

EP-205   1.5   R   1 HH-46D

Goal. Conduct emergency procedure familiarization.

Requirement

(1) Brief/Discuss. Differences between HH-46D/E and CH-46E aircraft.

(2) Introduce/Review

(a) All familiarization maneuvers with emphasis on hover and in-flight single engine emergencies.

(b) Perform practice autorotations and practice single engine flight.

(c) All emergency procedures/system failures.

Performance Standard. Pilot shall demonstrate knowledge of aircraft systems, perform basic FAM maneuvers, and be able to satisfactorily perform emergency procedures per NATOPS.

3. Instruments

a. Purpose. Develop proficiency in instrument flight procedures peculiar to the HH-46D/E aircraft under simulated or actual instrument conditions using all navigation aids.

b. General. All instrument flights will be conducted under actual or simulated instrument conditions.

c. Prerequisite. None.

d. Crew Requirements. IP/PUI/CC.

e. Flight Training (3 Flights, 4.5 Hours)

INST-210   1.5   SC,R   1 HH-46E   (N)

Goal. Review basic instrument and radio instrument procedures.

Requirement

(1) Discuss

(a) Local instrument patterns.

(b) Approach criteria.

(2) Introduce/Review

(a) Basic instrument work.

(b) Precision approaches to include ILS.

(c) Non-precision approaches.

Performance Standard. Pilot shall be able to perform basic instrument procedures per NATOPS Manual and Instrument Flight Manual, and radio instrument procedures per the Instrument Flight Manual.

INST-211   1.5   R   1 HH-46D   (N)

Goal. Review basic instrument and radio instrument procedures.

Requirement

(1) Discuss

(a) AN/ARC-182, CDI, and TACAN set up.

(b) Local instrument patterns.

(c) Approach criteria.

(2) Introduce/Review

(a) Basic instrument work.

(b) Precision approaches.

(c) Non-precision approaches.

Performance Standard. Pilot shall be able to perform basic instrument procedures per NATOPS Manual and Instrument Flight Manual, and radio instrument procedures per the Instrument Flight Manual.

INST-212   1.5   R   1 HH-46D   (N)

Goal. Practice radio instruments.

Requirement

(1) Brief/Discuss. Visual illusions and vertigo.

(2) Review

(a) RADAR approaches.

(b) Instrument navigation.

(c) Appropriate emergency procedures.

Performance Standard. Pilot shall be able to conduct radio instrument procedures and remain within the standards set forth in the Instrument Flight Manual.

4. Confined Area Landings

a. Purpose. Develop the ability to perform takeoffs and landings in confined areas.

b. Crew Requirements. IP/PUI/CC.

c. Flight Training (1 Flights, 1.5 Hours)

CAL-220   1.5   R   1 HH-46D/E

Goal. Conduct day confined area landings.

Requirement

(1) Brief/Discuss

(a) Normal and emergency procedures.

(b) Powerline and wire hazard proximity.

(c) Emergency vehicle locations.

(d) Crew coordination as they relate to CAL approaches.

(2) Review

(a) Normal Approach.

(b) Precision approach.

(c) Hover/No-hover landings.

Performance Standard. Pilot shall fly pattern within 50 ft and 10 kts of briefed altitude and airspeed, fly established pattern checkpoints, recognize closure rate to landing point remain oriented in zone, demonstrate power management maintain safe obstacle clearance, and land within one rotor of intended point of landing.

5. Fire Fighting

   a. Purpose. Develop the ability to conduct water bucket operations.

   b. Crew Requirements. IP/PUI/CC.

   c. Flight Training (1 FlighB 1.5 Hours)

FF-240   1.5   R   1 HH-46D/E

Goal. Develop water bucket operations proficiency.

Requirement

(1) Brief/Discuss

   (a) Water bucket pickup and release procedures.

   (b) Crew coordination.

   (c) ICS voice procedures.

   (d) Lost communications hand signals.

   (e) Emergency procedures.

   (f) Maximum HOGE weight for pickup and delivery and flight envelopes with water buckets.

   (g) Water bucket delivery techniques.

(2) Introduce. Water bucket operations.

(3) Review

   (a) Hover check.

   (b) All modes of cargo hook operation.

Performance Standard. Pilot shall fly pattern within 50 ft and 10 kts of briefed altitude and airspeed, fly established pattern checkpoints, properly respond to crew positioning calls, and maintain situational awareness of obstacles. Pilot shall be able to safely hold extended hover operations to fill Bambi Bucket demonstrate understanding of HIGE/HOGE requirements, complete minimum of 5 pickups and water drops, and deliver water to fire within 5 meters of intended point of impact.

6. Day Search and Rescue

    a. Purpose. Develop proficiency in Day Search and Rescue operations and navigation, to include search planning, search patterns and techniques, Doppler approach procedures, overland and over water rescue/recovery procedures.

    b. Prerequisites

        (1) The following flights of the Core Skill Basic phase shall be satisfactorily completed prior to commencement of Day SAR Core Skill Basic qualification training:

            (a) FAM-203

            (b) EP-204/205

            (c) CAL-220

        (2) Pilots may be designated as HH-46D/E (non-SAR) HAC at the discretion of the unit commanding officer prior to completion of the day and/or night SAR syllabi. Pilots who have not completed the appropriate SAR syllabus (day or night) shall not be assigned to SAR duty (day or night) until completion of the appropriate syllabus. Local commands are granted the authority to designate pilots as Day SAR HAC qualified upon completion of the Day Search and Rescue syllabus (see paragraph 109).

        (3) The following ground training shall be completed prior to commencing the Day SAR syllabus:

            (a) Search planning, to include local geographic and weather factors, parachute drift, water currents, sweep width, track space, probability of detection, and search patterns.

            (b) Utilization and limitations of SAR equipment.

            (c) SAR publications and directives.

            (d) Map study of the local area including landmarks, medical facilities, course rules, and landing areas.

            (e) SAR Coordinator, SAR Mission Commander, and On-scene Commander duties and responsibilities.

            (f) Local SAR organizations and their relationships.

            (g) Familiarity with local tactical and Air Traffic Control agencies and their capabilities and frequencies.

            (h) Legal implications of Search and Rescue.

            (i) GPS operation and limitations.

            (j) SAR Open Book Examination.

        (4) CRM shall be briefed for each syllabus flight.

7. Search And Rescue Navigation and Recovery Procedures

    a. Purpose. Develop proficiency in conducting search operations using additional navigation aids as available.

    b. General. The training is designed around local GPS capabilities. Differences in configurations and equipment will require modifications at each SAR command. Lack of appropriate equipment is sufficient basis for waiver of these syllabus flights.

    c. Crew Requirements. IP/PUI/CC/IFMT/RAC.

    d. Flight Training (10 Flights, 15.5 Hours)

SAR-250   1.5   SC,R   1 HH-46E

          Goal. Conduct GPS/dead reckoning navigation training.

          Requirement

          (1) Brief/Discuss

               (a) Aircraft GPS operation and programming.

               (b) Hand-held GPS operation and programming.

               (c) Dead reckoning principles.

               (d) Crew responsibilities.

               (e) Desired track, actual track, cross track, and CDI sensitivity.

               (f) CRM.

               (g) Time/distance checks.

               (h) Distance estimation and map information.

               (i) Map preparation.

               (j) Lost plane procedures.

          (2) Introduce

               (a) Dead reckoning procedures, emphasizing use of terrain, contour features, and triangulation to determine position.

               (b) GPS navigation procedures emphasizing use of secondary systems and dead reckoning as backup navigation.

               (c) Conduct a flight consisting of a minimum of 5 checkpoints at SAR altitudes (300-500 ft AGL). Remain within 500 meters of course line.

               (d) Enroute checklist.

          Performance Standard. Pilot shall input navigation route into GPS and shall fly a route consisting of a minimum of 5 checkpoints, maintain within 500 meters of course line, altitude within 50 feet and airspeed within 10 knots.

SAR-251   1.5   R   1 HH-46D

Goal. Conduct GPS/dead reckoning navigation training.

Requirement

(1) Brief/Discuss

    (a) Aircraft GPS operation and programming.

    (b) Hand-held GPS operation and programming.

    (c) Dead reckoning principles.

    (d) Crew responsibilities.

    (e) Desired track, actual track, cross track, and CDI sensitivity.

    (f) CRM.

    (g) Time/distance checks.

    (h) Distance estimation and map information.

    (i) Map preparation.

    (j) Lost plane procedures.

(2) Introduce

    (a) Dead reckoning procedures, emphasizing use of terrain, contour features, and triangulation to determine position.

    (b) GPS navigation procedures emphasizing use of secondary systems and dead reckoning as backup navigation.

    (c) Conduct a flight consisting of a minimum of 5 checkpoints at SAR altitudes (300-500 ft AGL). Remain within 500 meters of course line.

    (d) Enroute checklist.

Performance Standard. Pilot shall input navigation route into GPS and shall conduct a flight consisting of a minimum of 5 checkpoints, maintain within 500 meters of course line, altitude within 50 feet and airspeed within 10 knots.

SAR-252   1.5   R   1 HH-46D/E

Goal. Conduct search pattern and overland search procedures.

Requirement

(1) Brief/Discuss

    (a) Search patterns.

(b) Commence Search Point (CSP).

(c) Parallel track offset.

(d) Survivor signaling capabilities.

(e) Utilization of GPS to conduct search patterns.

(f) Multiple survivor location and assessment.

(g) Overland crewman deployment and pickup procedures.

(2) Introduce

(a) Search pattern execution using GPS.

(b) Parallel search pattern.

(c) Trackline search pattern.

(d) Pre-approach Doppler Checklist.

(3) Review

(a) Point-to-point navigation.

(b) Dead reckoning navigation.

(c) Confined area landings (CAL).

Performance Standard. Pilot shall input search pattern into GPS and shall conduct a search pattern consisting of a minimum of 5 checkpoints, maintain within 500 meters of course line, altitude within 50 feet and airspeed within 10 knots. Pilot shall conduct a hover for crewmember deployment maintaining within 10 feet of altitude, and within 5 feet of hover point.

SAR-253   1.5   R   1 HH-46D/E

Goal. Conduct day overland hoisting.

Requirement

(1) Brief/Discuss

(a) Crew responsibilities.

(b) Voice procedures and standard voice calls.

(c) Hand/arm signals.

(d) Emergency procedures and ICS failures during hover/hoist operations.

(e) Hoist limitations.

(f) Training requirements/limitations for overland hoisting.

(2) <u>Introduce</u>

    (a) Configure aircraft for hoisting operations.

    (b) Approach to pickup.

    (c) Hover positions/techniques.

        <u>1</u> Standby position/altitude.

        <u>2</u> Delivery/pickup position/altitude.

    (d) Hand/arm signals.

    (e) Gear delivery procedures.

    (f) Confined area delivery/pickup techniques.

<u>Performance Standard</u>. Pilot shall conduct a hover for crewmember deployment remaining within 10 feet of altitude and within 5 feet of hover point.

SAR-254   1.5   R   1 HH-46D/E

<u>Goal</u>. Conduct day overland, over-the-ramp hoisting.

<u>Requirement</u>

(1) <u>Brief/Discuss</u>

    (a) Crew responsibilities.

    (b) Voice procedures and standard voice calls.

    (c) Hand/arm signals.

    (d) Emergency procedures and ICS failures during hover/hoist operations.

    (e) Winch limitations.

    (f) Training requirements/limitations for overland hoisting.

(2) <u>Introduce</u>

    (a) Configure aircraft for over-the-ramp hoisting operations.

    (b) Hover positions/techniques.

        <u>1</u> Standby position/altitude.

        <u>2</u> Delivery/pickup position/altitude.

(3) <u>Review</u>

    (a) Hand/arm signals.

    (b) Gear delivery procedures.

(c) Confined area delivery/pickup techniques.

Performance Standard. Pilot shall conduct a hover for crewmember deployment remaining within 10 feet of altitude and within 5 feet of hover point.

Prerequisite. SAR-253.

SAR-255   2.0   R   1 HH-46D/E

Goal. Conduct day overland SAREX.

Requirement

(1) Brief/Discuss

    (a) SAR duty crew requirements, limitations, and Alert Conditions.

    (b) Short-fused information collection.

    (c) Mission Update Briefing techniques.

    (d) Aircraft configuration.

    (e) SAR equipment.

    (f) Coordinating agencies.

    (g) Use of SAR TACAID.

    (h) Emergency procedures.

(2) Introduce

    (a) Emergency response/recall procedures.

    (b) Scenario-based overland SAR Exercise.

(3) Review

    (a) SAR aircraft configurations.

    (b) Search patterns.

    (c) Hoisting operations.

    (d) Hover position/techniques.

    (e) Hand/arm signals.

    (f) Gear delivery procedures.

    (g) Confined area delivery/pickup techniques.

Performance Standard. Pilot shall navigate to a CSP, input search pattern into GPS and conduct a search pattern consisting of a minimum of 5 checkpoints, maintain within 500 meters of course line, altitude within 50 feet and airspeed within 10 knots. Pilot shall safely execute confined area landing, landing within 1 rotor of intended point of landing.

Pilot shall conduct a hover for crewmember deployment remaining within 10 feet of altitude, and within 5 feet of hover point.

Prerequisite. SAR-250/251, SAR-252, SAR-253.

External Syllabus Support. Hospital/LZ coordination as required for scenario. Survivors as required.

SAR-256   1.5   SC,R   1 HH-46E

Goal. Conduct day over water search and Doppler approaches.

Requirement

(1) Brief/Discuss

    (a) Procedures for sighting victims.

    (b) Use of flare for wind direction/speed determination.

    (c) Ditching procedures/considerations.

    (d) Crew responsibilities.

    (e) Remote flight control station operation and voice procedures.

    (f) Saltwater encrustation.

(2) Introduce

    (a) Flare deployment.

    (b) Sector search pattern.

    (c) Square search pattern.

    (d) Doppler approach pattern.

    (e) Conduct minimum of 3 manual and 3 coupled approaches.

    (f) Remote flight control station operation.

(3) Review

    (a) Hover positions/techniques

        1 Standby position/altitude.

        2 Deliver/pickup position/altitude.

    (b) Point-to-point navigation.

    (c) Dead reckoning navigation.

Performance Standard. Pilot shall input search pattern into GPS and shall conduct a search pattern consisting of a minimum of 5 checkpoints, maintain within 500 meters of course line, altitude within 50 feet and airspeed within 10 knots. Pilot shall conduct minimum of 3 manual and 3 coupled Doppler approaches, and shall maintain a hover for crewmember deployment remaining within 10 feet of altitude and within 5 feet of hover point.

Ordnance. 1 Mk-25 Flare, 1 Mk-58 Flare.

SAR-257   1.5   R   1 HH-46D

Goal. Conduct day over water search and approaches.

Requirement

(1) Brief/Discuss

    (a) Procedures for sighting victims.

    (b) Use of flare for wind direction/speed determination.

    (c) Ditching procedures/considerations.

    (d) Crew responsibilities.

    (e) Remote flight control station operation and voice procedures.

    (f) Saltwater encrustation.

(2) Introduce

    (a) Flare deployment.

    (b) Sector search pattern.

    (c) Square search pattern.

    (d) Doppler approach pattern.

    (e) Conduct minimum of 3 manual and 3 coupled approaches.

    (f) Remote flight control station operation.

(3) Review

    (a) Hover positions/techniques

        1 Standby position/altitude.

        2 Deliver/pickup position/altitude.

    (b) Point-to-point navigation.

    (c) Dead reckoning navigation.

Performance Standard. Pilot shall input search pattern into GPS and shall conduct a search pattern consisting of a minimum of 5 checkpoints, maintain within 500 meters of course line, altitude within 50 feet and airspeed within 10 knots. Pilot shall conduct minimum of 3 manual and 3 coupled Doppler approaches, and shall maintain a hover for crewmember deployment remaining within 10 feet of altitude and within 5 feet of hover point.

Ordnance. 1 Mk-25 Flare, 1 Mk-58 Flare.

SAR-258   1.5   R   1 HH-46D/E

Goal. Conduct day maritime SAR training (Water works).

Requirement

(1) Brief/Discuss

(a) Crew responsibilities.

(b) Rescue Air Crewman (RAC) deployment altitudes and procedures.

(c) RAC safety, environmental, debris, and predator considerations.

(d) Rescue equipment and trail line operation.

(e) Procedures for loss of visual contact with RAC.

(f) Short haul procedures.

(2) Introduce

(a) RAC deployment.

(b) Rescue equipment deployment and recovery.

(c) Short haul procedures.

(d) RAC and survivor recovery.

(3) Review

(a) Flare deployment.

(b) Doppler approach pattern.

(c) Manual and coupled approaches.

(d) Hover positions/techniques.

Performance Standard. Pilot shall conduct a hover for crewmember deployment maintaining within 10 feet of altitude and within 5 feet of hover point. Pilot shall conduct a short haul of at least 500 meters remaining within 10 feet of safe short haul altitude and placing rescue air crewman within 10 feet of intended point of landing.

Prerequisite. SAR-253, SAR-256/257.

Ordnance. 1 Mk-25 Flare, 1 Mk-58 Flare.

External Syllabus Support. Safety Boat/aircraft with safety swimmer. Survivors as required.

SAR-260   1.5   R   1 HH-46D/E

Goal. Conduct day boat hoist. (If practical, IP should demo from right seat then hot seat crew positions for introduction items. For safety, the Pilot-At-Controls (PAC) shall be the right seat pilot for the approach-to-boat and over-the-boat operations.)

Requirement

(1) Brief/Discuss

   (a) Crew responsibilities.

   (b) Approach-to-boat.

   (c) Hover position, altitude, and scan.

   (d) Voice procedures.

   (e) RAC deployment considerations.

   (f) ORM/safety considerations.

   (g) Rescue equipment and trail line operation.
   (h) Loss of visual contact with boat.

   (i) Emergency procedures over the boat.

(2) Demonstrate

   (a) Approach-to-boat.

   (b) Hover position/altitude.

   (c) RAC and survivor recovery.

(3) Introduce

   (a) Approach-to-boat.

   (b) Hover position/altitude.
   (c) RAC and survivor deployment and recovery.

   (d) Rescue equipment deployment and recovery.

   (e) Short haul procedures.

Performance Standard. Pilot shall conduct a minimum of 3 approaches to a boat configured for SAR rescue, and conduct a hover for crewmember deployment maintaining within 10 feet of altitude and within 5 feet of hover point. Pilot shall conduct "back and left" maneuvers in conjunction with approaches remaining within 50 meters of the boat. A minimum of 3 hoists from the deck of the boat shall be conducted.

Prerequisite. SAR-253, SAR-256/257, SAR-258.

External Syllabus Support. Safety Boat suitable for hoisting personnel to/from, with safety swimmer. Survivors as required.

132. CORE SKILL ADVANCED TRAINING

1. Night Vision Goggles

    a. Purpose. Develop proficiency in conducting basic familiarization and navigation operations using NVGs.

    b. General. Search and Rescue NSQ consists of NVG-300 through SAR-340.

    c. Prerequisites. The Night Operations Course contained in the MAWTS-1 Course Catalog as well as the following flights shall be completed prior to commencing the NVG syllabus.

        (1) FAM-203

        (2) EP-204, 205

        (3) INST-210, 211

        (4) CAL-220

    d. Crew Requirement. NSSI/PUI/CC/O.

    e. Flight Training (4 Flights, 6.0 Hours)

NVG-300   1.5   R   1 HH-46D/E   NS

        Goal. NVG familiarization flight in HLL conditions.

        Requirement

        (1) Brief/Discuss

            (a) Crew coordination.

            (b) Crew comfort levels.

            (c) NVG operations and limitations.

            (d) Emergency procedures.

            (e) Differences between HH-46D and CH-46E.

        (2) Introduce

            (a) Use of NVGs at an unlit field.

            (b) Use of NVGs while performing taxi, basic low work, and normal takeoffs/landings.

            (c) Touch and go landings with emphasis on aircraft control and cockpit coordination.

        Performance Standard. Pilot shall maintain effective NVG/instrument scan, recognize closure rate with intended point of landing, retain positive aircraft control, demonstrate effective cockpit management utilize proper terminology, fly pattern within 50 feet and 10 kts of briefed altitude and airspeed, fly established pattern checkpoints and land within 1 rotor of intended point of landing.

NVG-301   1.5   R   1 HH-46D/E   NS

Goal. Develop proficiency in confined area landings using NVGs. This flight may be conducted in HLL or LLL conditions.

Requirement

(1) Brief/Discuss

    (a) Crew Coordination.

    (b) Crew comfort levels.

    (c) Aircraft lighting.

    (d) Confined area landing approaches.

    (e) Scanning techniques.

(2) Introduce

    (a) Confined area takeoff and landings using NVGs.
    (b) Plan/navigate a route to a confined area landing site.

    (c) Enroute to a CAL site demonstrate the difficulty of terrain reference at altitude.

Performance Standard. Pilot shall maintain effective NVG/instrument scan, recognize closure rate with intended point of landing, retain positive aircraft control, demonstrate effective cockpit management utilize proper terminology, fly pattern within 50 feet and 10 kts of briefed altitude and airspeed, fly established pattern checkpoints, remain oriented in zone, and land within 1 rotor of intended point of landing.

Prerequisite. NVG-300.

NVG-302   1.5   R   1 HH-46D/E   NS

Goal. Develop proficiency in low level navigation operations using NVGs. This flight may be conducted in HLL or LLL conditions.

Requirement

(1) Brief/Discuss

    (a) CRM.

    (b) Crew comfort levels.

    (c) Aircraft lighting.

    (d) Navigation and search altitudes.

(e) Scanning techniques.

(f) Emergency procedures relating to low level NVG operations.

(2) Introduce

(a) Low level navigation.

(b) Navigation from a confined area landing site to a hospital landing pad.

(c) Obstacles along route of flight.

Performance Standard. Pilot shall input a navigation route into GPS and conduct an NVG flight consisting of a minimum of 5 checkpoints, maintain effective NVG/instrument scan, recognize proper closure rate with intended point of landing, remain oriented on route within 500 meters, ensure effective CRM for navigation and obstacle clearance, retain positive aircraft control, and demonstrate effective cockpit management for precision navigation utilizing proper terminology.

Prerequisite. NVG-300.

2. Night Search and Rescue

a. Purpose

(1) Develop proficiency in night Search and Rescue operations to include search planning, search patterns and techniques, Doppler approach procedures, over water and overland rescue/recovery procedures.

(2) Pilots may fly the night SAR syllabus codes with or without the aid of Night Vision Devices (NVD). The intent of this syllabus is to develop the skills critical to the Search and Rescue mission versus NVD proficiency. NVD proficiency/currency should be considered when conducting NVD SAR flights.

(3) When complete with the night SAR training syllabus, aircrew should have the ability to conduct night SAR missions under various atmospheric conditions.

b. Prerequisites

(1) Pilots may begin the night SAR syllabus training prior to completion of the entire day SAR syllabus. Prior to commencement of a night

SAR syllabus flight the corresponding day SAR syllabus flight shall be complete.

(2) The pilot must have completed the NVG syllabus.

(3) Initial syllabus training flights utilizing NVDs shall be flown with a Night Systems SAR Instructor (NSSI).

c. Crew Requirements. IP/PUI/CC/IFMT/RAC. (Designated NSSI and NSQ HLL/LLL for flights utilizing NVDs.)

d. Flight Training (8 flights, 13.0 hours)

NSAR-320   1.5   R   1 HH-46D/E   N

Goal. Conduct night over land search.

Requirement

(1) Brief/Discuss

    (a) Search patterns.

    (b) Commence Search Point (CSP).

    (c) Parallel track offset.

    (d) Survivor signaling capabilities at night.

    (e) Multiple survivor location and assessment.

    (f) Overland crewman deployment and pickup procedures.

(2) Introduce

    (a) Search patterns.

    (b) Night Sun use and techniques.

    (c) Signaling devices.

(3) Review. Night CALs.

Performance Standard. Pilot shall input search pattern into
GPS and shall conduct a search pattern consisting of a minimum
of 5 checkpoints, maintain within 500 meters of course line,
altitude within 50 feet and airspeed within 10 knots.

Prerequisite. SAR-252.

NSAR-321   1.5   R   1 HH-46D/E   N

Goal. Conduct night overland hoisting.

Requirement

(1) Brief/Discuss

    (a) Crew responsibilities.

    (b) Voice procedures and standard voice calls.

    (c) Hand/arm signals at night.

    (d) Emergency procedures during hover/hoist operations.

    (e) Maneuvering aircraft over survivor at night.

(2) Introduce

    (a) Configure aircraft for night hoisting operations.

    (b) Approach to pickup.

    (c) Hover positions/techniques.

       <u>1</u> Standby position/altitude.

       <u>2</u> Delivery/pickup position/altitude.

    (d) Night hand/arm signals.

    (e) Night gear delivery procedures.

    (f) Confined area delivery/pickup techniques.

(3) <u>Review</u>

    (a) Gear delivery procedures.

    (b) Confined area delivery/pickup techniques.

    (c) Night CALs.

<u>Performance Standard</u>. Pilot shall safely conduct confined area landing, landing within 1 rotor of intended point of landing. Pilot shall conduct a hover for crewmember deployment maintaining within 10 feet of altitude, and within 5 feet of hover point.

<u>Prerequisite</u>. SAR-253.

NSAR-322   2.0   R   1 HH-46D/E   N

<u>Goal</u>. Conduct night overland SAREX.

<u>Requirement</u>

(1) <u>Brief/Discuss</u>

    (a) SAR duty crew requirements, limitations, and Alert Conditions.

    (b) Short-fused information collection.

    (c) Mission Update Briefing techniques.

    (d) Aircraft configuration.

    (e) SAR equipment.

    (f) Coordinating agencies.

    (g) Use of SAR TACAID.

    (h) Emergency Procedures.

(2) <u>Introduce</u>

    (a) Night emergency response/recall procedures.

    (b) Night scenario-based overland SAR Exercise.

(3) <u>Review</u>

    (a) SAR aircraft configurations.

    (b) Search patterns.

    (c) Hoisting operations.

    (d) Hover position/techniques.

    (e) Night hand/arm signals.

    (f) Night gear delivery procedures.

    (g) Night confined area delivery/pickup techniques.

<u>Performance Standard</u>. Pilot shall input search pattern into GPS and shall conduct a search pattern consisting of a minimum of 5 checkpoints, maintain within 500 meters of course line, altitude within 50 feet and airspeed within 10 knots. Pilot shall safely conduct confined area landing, landing within 1 rotor of intended point of landing. Pilot shall conduct a hover for crewmember deployment maintaining within 10 feet of altitude, and within 5 feet of hover point.

<u>Prerequisite</u>. SAR-255, NSAR-320, NSAR-321.

<u>External Syllabus Support</u>. Hospital/LZ coordination as required for scenario. Survivors as required.

NSAR-323   1.5   SC,R   1 HH-46E   N

<u>Goal</u>. Conduct night over water SAR approaches.

<u>Requirement</u>

(1) <u>Brief/Discuss</u>

    (a) Procedures for sighting victims at night.

    (b) Use of flare at night.

    (c) Ditching procedures/considerations.

    (d) Crew responsibilities.

    (e) Night instrument scan/low visibility operations in close proximity to the water.

    (f) Coupled Doppler system.

    (g) Saltwater encrustation.

(2) <u>Introduce</u>

    (a) Night flare deployment.

    (b) Sector search pattern.

    (c) Square search pattern.

(d) Doppler approach pattern.

(e) Conduct minimum of 3 manual and 3 coupled approaches.

(f) Remote flight control station operation.

(3) Review

(a) Hover positions/techniques

<u>1</u> Standby position/altitude.

<u>2</u> Deliver/pickup position/altitude.

(b) Point-to-point navigation.

(c) Dead Reckoning navigation.

Performance Standard. Pilot shall input search pattern into GPS and shall conduct a search pattern consisting of a minimum of 5 checkpoints, maintain within 500 meters of course line, altitude within 50 feet and airspeed within 10 knots. Pilot shall conduct minimum of 3 manual and 3 coupled Doppler approaches, and shall maintain a hover for crewmember deployment remaining within 10 feet of altitude, and within 5 feet of hover point.

Prerequisite. SAR-256

Ordnance. 1 Mk-25 Flare, 1 Mk-58 Flare.

NSAR-324   1.5   R   1 HH-46D   N

Goal. Conduct night over water SAR approaches.

Requirement

(1) Brief/Discuss

(a) Procedures for sighting victims at night.

(b) Use of flare at night.

(c) Ditching procedures/considerations.

(d) Crew responsibilities.

(e) Night instrument scan/low visibility operations in close proximity to the water.

(f) Coupled Doppler system.

(g) Saltwater encrustation.

(2) Introduce

(a) Night flare deployment.

(b) Sector search pattern.

(c) Square search pattern.

(d) Doppler approach pattern.

(e) Conduct minimum of 3 manual and 3 coupled approaches.

(f) Remote flight control station operation.

(3) Review

    (a) Hover positions/techniques

        1 Standby position/altitude.

        2 Deliver/pickup position/altitude.

    (b) Point-to-point navigation.

    (c) Dead Reckoning navigation.

Performance Standard. Pilot shall input search pattern into GPS and shall conduct a search pattern consisting of a minimum of 5 checkpoints, maintain within 500 meters of course line, altitude within 50 feet and airspeed within 10 knots. Pilot shall conduct minimum of 3 manual and 3 coupled Doppler approaches, and shall maintain a hover for crewmember deployment remaining within 10 feet of altitude, and within 5 feet of hover point.

Prerequisite. SAR-257

Ordnance. 1 Mk-25 Flare, 1 Mk-58 Flare.

NSAR-330   1.5   R   1 HH-46D/E   N

Goal. Conduct night rescue swimmer deployment (Night water works).

Requirement

(1) Brief/Discuss

    (a) Crew responsibilities.

    (b) Rescue Air Crewman (RAC) deployment altitudes and procedures.

    (c) RAC safety, environmental, debris, and predator considerations.

    (d) Rescue equipment and trail line operation.

    (e) Procedures for loss of visual contact with RAC at night.

    (f) Short haul procedures.

(2) Introduce

    (a) RAC deployment.

(b) Rescue equipment deployment and recovery.

(c) RAC and survivor recovery.

(3) Review

(a) Flare deployment.

(b) Doppler approach pattern.

(c) Manual and coupled approaches.

(d) Hover positions/techniques.

Performance Standard. Pilot shall conduct a hover for crewmember deployment maintaining within 10 feet of altitude, and within 5 feet of hover point. Pilot shall conduct a short haul of at least 100 meters remaining within 10 feet of safe short haul altitude and placing rescue air crewman within 10 feet of intended point of landing.

Prerequisite. SAR-258, NSAR-320, NSAR-321, NSAR-323/324.

Ordnance. 1 Mk-25 Flare, 1 Mk-58 Flare.

External Syllabus Support. Safety boat/aircraft with safety swimmer. Survivors as required.

NSAR-333   1.5   R   1 HH-46D/E   N

Goal. Conduct night SAR boat hoist. (If practical, IP should demo from right seat then hot seat crew positions for introduction items. For safety, the pilot-at-controls (PAC) should be the right seat pilot for the approach to boat and over-the-boat operations.)

Requirement

(1) Brief/Discuss

(a) Crew responsibilities.

(b) Boat lighting/antennas.

(c) Approach to boat.

(d) Hover position, altitude, and scan.

(e) Voice procedures.

(f) RAC deployment considerations.
(g) ORM/safety considerations.

(h) Rescue equipment and trail line operation.

(i) Loss of visual contact with boat at night.

(j) Emergency procedures over the boat at night.

    (2) <u>Demonstrate</u>

        (a) Approach to boat.

        (b) Hover position/altitude.

        (c) RAC and survivor recovery.

    (3) <u>Introduce</u>

        (a) Approach to boat.

        (b) Hover position/altitude.

        (c) RAC and survivor deployment and recovery.

        (d) Rescue equipment deployment and recovery.

        (e) Short haul procedures.

<u>Performance Standard</u>. Pilot shall conduct a minimum of 3 approaches to a boat configured for SAR rescue, and conduct a hover for crewmember deployment maintaining within 10 feet of altitude, and within 5 feet of hover point. Pilot shall conduct "back and left" maneuvers in conjunction with approaches remaining within 50 meters of the boat. A minimum of 3 hoists from the deck of the boat shall be conducted.

<u>Prerequisite</u>. SAR-260, NSAR-330.

<u>External Syllabus Support</u>. Safety boat suitable for hoisting personnel to/from, with safety swimmer. Survivors as required.

NSAR-340   2.0   <u>R</u>   1 HH-46D/E   <u>N</u>

<u>Goal</u>. Conduct night over water SAREX to integrate all skills learned in the day and night SAR syllabi to affect a search, recovery and delivery of a survivor or survivors to competent medical care.

<u>Requirement</u>

(1) <u>Brief/Discuss</u>. Scenario based SAR evolution. IP should provide the PUI with a scenario and brief/discuss limitations

and safety as it pertains to deployment and recovery of aircrew during training evolutions.

(2) <u>Review</u>

    (a) Launch on a simulated SAR mission, either overland or over water, or a combination. PUI shall be given a scenario and be required to develop a plan and brief the crew prior to launching using SOP readiness and launch criteria.

    (b) Short-fused information collection and planning.

    (c) Emergency response/recall procedures.

(d) Any search pattern.

(e) Conduct manual and coupled approaches.

(f) Deploy/recover aircrew and survivors.

(g) Hoisting operations.

Performance Standard. Pilot shall complete a successful search (overland or over water), conduct hoist recovery operations, and delivery of patient to competent medical care.

Prerequisite. Day SAR syllabus complete. NVG syllabus complete. Night SAR syllabus complete through NSAR-333.

Ordnance. 1 Mk-25 Flare, 1 Mk-58 Flare.

External Syllabus Support. Hospital/LZ coordination as required for scenario. Safety boat/aircraft with safety swimmer as required. Survivors as required.

133. CORE PLUS TRAINING

1. Helicopter Inland Rescue Air Crewman (HIRA) Rappel Operations

   a. Purpose. Develop proficiency in rappelling procedures.

   b. General

   (1) All rappel training evolutions shall be conducted with the use of a belay line for "bagless" rappels or have a HIRA qualified safety observer tending the free end of the rappel rope during the "standard" rappel.

   (2) Only HIRA qualified personnel shall act as survivor for all HIRA training short haul evolutions.

   c. Prerequisites. CAL-220, SAR-253.

   d. Crew Requirements. IP/PUI/CC/HIRAI/HTRAUT

   e. Flight Training (1 flight 1.5 hours)

RAP-402   1.5   R   1 HH-46D/E

      Goal. Conduct SAR rappelling and short haul operations.

      Requirement

      (1) Brief/Discuss

         (a) Crew responsibilities.

         (b) Voice procedures and standard voice calls.

         (c) Hand/arm signals.

         (d) Emergency procedures during rappel operations.

         (e) Rappelling with equipment and litter short haul procedures.

(f) Training requirements/limitations for overland hoisting.

(2) <u>Introduce/Demonstrate</u>

(a) Configure aircraft for rappelling operations.

(b) Conduct minimum of 3 rappel descents with equipment.

(c) Minimum of 2 descents should end with short haul of a simulated survivor in rescue litter.

(d) Hand/arm signals.

<u>Performance Standard</u>. Pilot shall safely conduct confined area landing, landing within 10 feet of intended point of landing. Pilot shall conduct a hover for crewmember rappel deployment maintaining within 10 feet of altitude, and within 5 feet of hover point and conduct a short haul of at least 500 meters remaining within 10 feet of safe short haul altitude and placing rescue air crewman within 10 feet of intended point of landing.

<u>Prerequisite</u>. CAL-220, SAR-253

2. <u>Carrier Qualification</u>

a. <u>Purpose</u>. Qualify during day and night shipboard landings.

b. <u>General</u>. Training includes FCLP/CQ and NVG operations. Over water searches may require shipboard operations for refueling, casualty recovery, and/or remote site launches. Pilots should be familiar with aviation capable ships to support that contingency. The benefits of NVG operations cannot be overemphasized, and every effort should be made to ensure all crewmembers are SAR Night Systems Qualified (SAR NSQ). The CQ syllabus is designed as an NVG-centric syllabus, but all pilots should be familiar with unaided shipboard operations.

(1) Refer to the NATOPS Manual, NWP 3-04.1 (Helicopter Operations for Air Capable Ships), and LHA/LPH/LHD NATOPS.

(2) Pilots who are CQ current in the model H-46 helicopter will be considered current in the HH-46D/E until that currency expires.

(3) Five day and five NVD landings required for qualification/ currency.

c. <u>Crew Requirements</u>. IP/PUI/CC.

d. <u>Flight Training (4 Flights, 6.0 Hours)</u>

<u>FCLP-410</u>   1.5   R   1 HH-46D/E

<u>Goal</u>. Day Field Carrier Landing Pattern (FCLP) familiarization.

<u>Requirement</u>

(1) <u>Brief/Discuss</u>

(a) Aircrew coordination.

(b) Verbal/visual communications used during shipboard landings.

(c) LSE signals.

(d) Water landing/ditching.

(e) Aircraft lighting.

(2) <u>Introduce</u>

(a) Day FCLP patterns.

(b) Approaches and landings.

(c) Emergency procedures peculiar to shipboard operations.

<u>Performance Standard</u>. Pilot shall demonstrate proper shipboard communications and aircraft lighting procedures, maintain effective instrument scan, execute proper cockpit switchology, fly established CQ pattern demonstrating understanding of proper upwind, crosswind and interval parameters, fly 300 ft/80 kt pattern within 50 ft and 10 kts, maintain proper closure and bearing with intended ship landing spot respond promptly and safely to altitude and drift calls from aircrew, remain oriented on assigned landing spot and land within 1 meter of intended point of landing.

<u>External Syllabus Support.</u> Marked FCLP deck.

FCLP-411   1.5   R   1 HH-46D/E   NS

<u>Goal</u>. Night FCLP familiarization.

<u>Requirement</u>

(1) <u>Brief/Discuss</u>

(a) Aircrew coordination.

(b) Verbal/Visual communications used during shipboard landings.

(c) LSE signals.

(d) Water landing/ditching.

(e) Aircraft lighting.

(2) <u>Introduce</u>

(a) Night FCLP patterns.

(b) Minimum of 3 night FCLP landings will be conducted.

(c) Approaches and landings.

(d) Emergency procedures peculiar to shipboard operations.

Performance Standard. Pilot shall demonstrate proper shipboard communications and aircraft lighting procedures, maintain effective instrument scan, execute proper cockpit switchology, maintain effective NVG/instrument scan, fly established CQ pattern demonstrating understanding of proper upwind, crosswind and interval parameters, fly 300 ft/80 kt pattern within 50 ft and 10 kts, maintain proper closure and bearing with intended ship landing spot respond promptly and safely to altitude and drift calls from aircrew, remain oriented on assigned landing spot and land within 1 meter of intended point of landing.

Prerequisite. FCLP-410.

External Syllabus Support. Marked FCLP deck.

CQ-420   1.5   R   1 HH-46D/E

Goal. Day carrier qualification.

Requirement

(1) Brief/Discuss

   (a) Aircrew coordination.

   (b) Verbal/visual communications used during shipboard landings.

   (c) LSE signals.

   (d) Water landing/ditching.

   (e) Aircraft lighting.

(2) Introduce. Day carrier qualification per NATOPS.

Performance Standard. Pilot shall fly 300 ft/80 kt pattern within 25 ft and 10 kts, fly established CQ pattern demonstrating understanding of proper upwind, crosswind and interval parameters, maintain proper orientation to LSE, respond promptly and safely to altitude and drift calls from aircrew, remain oriented on assigned landing spot land within 1 meter of intended point of landing, utilize solid instrument scan, recognize proper closure rate with intended point of landing, demonstrate understanding of shipboard communications, and aircraft lighting.

Prerequisite. FCLP-410.

External Syllabus Support. Air capable ship deck.

CQ-421   1.5   R   1 HH-46D/E   NS

Goal. Night carrier qualification.

Requirement

(1) Brief/Discuss

(a) Aircrew coordination.

(b) Verbal/visual communications used during shipboard landings.

(c) Minimum of 3 night CQ landings will be conducted.

(d) LSE signals at night.

(e) Water landing/ditching and other aircraft emergencies relative to the night shipboard environment.

(f) Aircraft and shipboard lighting.

(g) NVG emergency procedures.

(h) Night alternate pattern.

(2) Introduce. Night carrier qualification per NATOPS.

Performance Standard. Pilot shall fly 300 ft/80 kt pattern within 25 ft and 10 kts, fly established CQ pattern demonstrating understanding of proper upwind, crosswind and interval parameters, maintain proper orientation to LSE, respond promptly and safely to altitude and drift calls from aircrew, remain oriented on assigned landing spot land within 1 meter of intended point of landing, utilize solid NVG/instrument scan, recognize proper closure rate with intended point of landing, demonstrate understanding of shipboard communications, and aircraft lighting.

Prerequisite. FCLP-411, CQ-420.

External Syllabus Support. Air capable ship deck.

140. INSTRUCTOR UNDER TRAINING (IUT): SAR NATOPS/ASSISTANT NATOPS INSTRUCTOR

1. Purpose. Develop qualified instructor pilots with the ability to teach SAR operations using standardized flight training.

2. General. Maneuver descriptions are found in the HMMT-164 H-46 Standardization Manual, NATOPS Flight Manual and the MAWTS-1 Course Catalog.

3. Prerequisite. Designated SAR HAC.

4. Crew Requirements. IP/IUT/CC/RAC/IFMT.

5. Training

a. Ground Training. IUTs will complete the appropriate portion of the ISD program and present 1 SAR class from the SAR Training Lectures CD prior to qualification.

b. Simulator Training. Incorporated in the flight training.

c. Flight Training (3 Flights, 6.0 Hours)

IUT-500   1.5   E   1 HH-46D/E

Goal. Demonstrate instructional techniques during day
FAM/EP/CAL maneuvers and procedures.

Requirement

(1) Brief/Discuss

    (a) Crew coordination.

    (b) Confined area landings.

    (c) Emergency procedures.

    (d) Instrument checklists.

    (e) Attitude instrument flight.

    (f) Instrument approaches.

    (g) Flight planning.

(2) Review

    (a) All FAM stage maneuvers.

    (b) Confined area landings.

    (c) Instrument procedures.

Performance Standard. Pilot shall demonstrate the ability to
instruct familiarization and instrument maneuvers, including
demonstrating and introducing maneuvers to pilots under
instruction.

IUT-503   1.5   E   1 HH-46D/E

Goal. Instructional water bucket operations and personnel
hoisting procedures.

Requirement

(1) Brief/Discuss

    (a) Crew coordination.

    (b) Load computation/planning.

    (c) Emergency procedures.

(2) Review

    (a) Water bucket operations.

    (b) External hoist operations.

    (c) Hoist operations using internal winch.

Performance Standard. Pilot shall demonstrate the ability to instruct water bucket operations maneuvers and delivery techniques, including demonstrating and introducing maneuvers to pilots under instruction.

IUT-504   3.0   E   1 HH-46D/E   (N)

Goal. Review all instructional techniques for SAR inflight procedures. This flight may be flown in a day or night environment.

Requirement

(1) Brief/Discuss

    (a) Aircraft configuration.

    (b) SAR equipment.

    (c) Coordinating agencies.

    (d) Flare patterns.

    (e) Use of SAR TACAID.

    (f) Crew coordination.

    (g) Emergency procedures.

(2) Review

    (a) LORAN navigation.

    (b) Search patterns.

    (c) Manual and coupled approaches.

    (d) Deployment of swimmer/corpsman.

    (e) Inland/Maritime survivor recovery.

    (f) Use of enroute checklists.

Performance Standard. Pilot shall demonstrate the ability to instruct Search and Rescue maneuvers, including demonstrating and introducing search patterns and techniques, and hover and recovery maneuvers to pilots under instruction.

Prerequisite. FAM-500, FF-503.

Ordnance. 4 MK-58 Flares as required.

141. INSTRUCTOR UNDER TRAINING (GRADUATE LEVEL: NSSI)

1. Pilots under instruction shall refer to the MAWTS-1 Course Catalog. There are no refly factors for these instructor flights.

2. An NSSI is a NA who has completed the NVG syllabus, certified by a NSI and designated by his squadron Commanding Officer. Designated NSSIs are qualified to instruct all SAR NVG flights.

3. The NSSI under training shall have completed IUT-500, 503, and 504 and have been designated an Assistant NATOPS Instructor or NATOPS Instructor.

4. <u>Flight Training (3 Flights, 6 hours)</u>

IUT-550   2.0   E   1 HH-46D/E   NS

       <u>Goal</u>. Conduct low work, pattern work, FAM maneuvers and simulated emergencies under HLL or LLL conditions.

       <u>Requirement</u>

       (1) <u>Brief/Discuss</u>

           (a) Use of NVD's, aircraft lighting (internal and external), emergency procedures, wave off procedures, inadvertent IMC and NVD failures.

           (b) Depth perception, visual illusions and scan techniques.

           (c) Crew coordination, comfort level, and situational awareness.

           (d) NVG training restrictions/requirements.

       (2) The IUT shall conduct with an emphasis on instructional technique, low work, FAM maneuvers, FCLPs and simulated emergencies.

       <u>Performance Standard</u>. Pilot shall demonstrate the ability to instruct pilots in the use of NVDs while conducting all FAM maneuvers and simulated emergencies.

IUT-551   2.0   E   1 HH-46D/E   NS

       <u>Goal</u>. Conduct CALs and navigation while utilizing NVGs under LLL conditions.

       <u>Requirement</u>

       (1) <u>Brief/Discuss</u>

           (a) Crew coordination and comfort level.

           (b) NVG considerations, NVG CAL techniques, LZ lighting, brown/white out NVG navigation techniques and NVG map preparation.

           (c) NVG enroute hazards and inadvertent IMC.

       (2) The IUT shall demonstrate, with emphasis on instructional technique, confined area landings and navigation of a route (50NM or greater) at or above 200 feet AGL. The IUT shall remain orientated within 200 meters.

       <u>Performance Standard</u>. Pilot shall demonstrate the ability to instruct pilots in the use of NVDs while conducting confined area landings.

IUT-552   2.0   E   1 HH-46D/E   NS

        Goal. Evaluate the IUTs ability to instruct CALs and navigation in a SAR environment while utilizing NVGs under LLL conditions.

        Requirement

        (1) Brief/Discuss. Review brief and discussion items from NVG 550 and 551.

        (2) The IUT shall demonstrate, with emphasis on instructional technique, confined area landings and navigation of route (50NM minimum) at or above 200 feet AGL in a SAR scenario.

        Performance Standard. Pilot shall demonstrate the ability to instruct pilots in the use of NVDs while conducting confined area landings.

        Prerequisite. IUT-550 and 551.

150. REQUIREMENTS, QUALIFICATIONS AND DESIGNATIONS

1. NATOPS and Instrument Evaluations

    a. Purpose. Determine if the pilot is qualified per the criteria contained in the H-46D/E NATOPS Flight Manual, OPNAVINST 3710.7, and applicable SAR publications.

    b. General. SAR check rides should coincide with the annual NATOPS evaluation to the maximum extent possible.

    c. Crew Requirements. IP/PUI/CC.

    d. Flight Training (6 Flights, 12.0 Hours)

RQD-600   1.5   E   1 HH-46D/E   (N)

        Goal. Annual NATOPS Evaluation.

        Requirement. Proficiency in the utilization of all aspects of the HH-46 as a system. The proficiency expected by the evaluator in this flight shall be commensurate with the experience of the pilot under evaluation. Upon successful completion of this evaluation, a pilot may be designated a HH-46D/E (non-SAR) HAC and/or SAR H2P at the discretion of the units commanding officer.

        Performance Standard. The performance expected by the evaluator in this flight shall be commensurate with the experience level of the pilot under evaluation.

RQD-601   1.5   E   1 HH-46D/E   (N)

        Goal. Annual Instrument Evaluation.

        Requirement. The evaluation shall be conducted per the criteria contained within the Instrument Flight Manual. File and fly an instrument round robin using all navigation equipment available. Evaluate all phases of instrument flight to include precision and non-precision approaches, partial panel, and instrument holding. Demonstrate proficiency in handling instrument related emergencies to include unusual attitude recoveries.

Performance Standard. Pilot shall demonstrate the ability to plan and execute an instrument flight conduct instrument approaches, and demonstrate safe performance in handling instrument related emergencies, including unusual attitudes.

RQD-602   3.0   E   1 HH-46D/E

Goal. Day SAR Evaluation. This flight may be flown in conjunction with an annual NATOPS evaluation (RQD-600).

Requirement. The check will be conducted per the criteria contained in the NATOPS Flight Manual, OPNAVINST 3710.7, applicable SAR publications, and will cover all practicable day SAR operations and procedures contained in this syllabus. Upon successful completion of this evaluation, a pilot may be designated Day SAR HAC at the discretion of the unit commanding officer.

Performance Standard. The performance expected by the evaluator in this flight shall be commensurate with the experience level of the pilot under evaluation.

RQD-603   3.0   E   1 HH-46D/E   N

Goal. Night SAR evaluation. This flight may be flown in conjunction with an annual NATOPS evaluation (RQD-600).

Requirement. The check will be conducted per the criteria contained in the NATOPS Flight Manual, OPNAVINST 3710.7, applicable SAR publications, and will cover all practicable night SAR operations and procedures contained in this syllabus. Upon successful completion of this evaluation, a pilot may be designated Full SAR Qualified HAC.

Performance Standard. The performance expected by the evaluator in this flight shall be commensurate with the experience level of the pilot under evaluation.

Ordnance. 1 Mk-25, 1 Mk-58 Flares.

RQD-604   1.5   E   1 HH-46D/E

Goal. Functional Check Pilot (FCP) Evaluation.

Requirement. Per a locally generated syllabus, conduct an evaluation with a previously designated FCP.

Performance Standard. Pilot shall demonstrate the ability to conduct a Full Card Functional Check Flight correctly and efficiently, and demonstrate the ability to troubleshoot aircraft problems.

Prerequisite. SAR-257/258.

RQD-640 1.5 E   1 HH-46D/E   (N)

    Goal. Annual Crew Resource Management (CRM) Evaluation.

    Requirement. The evaluation shall be conducted per the criteria contained within OPNAVINST 1542.7C. The flight evaluation may be conducted concurrent with any operational or training flight including NATOPS evaluation and/or instrument evaluation.

    Performance Standard. Demonstrate effective use of the 7 CRM critical skill areas.

160. TRAINING RESOURCES (ORDNANCE). The below ordnance requirements are based on a "per crew" basis per OPNAVNOTE 8010.

ORDNANCE	200 SERIES	300 SERIES	500 SERIES	600 SERIES	ANNUAL*
Mk-25 Flares	3	4	1	1	9
Mk-58 Flares	3	4	1	1	9

* Annual Ordnance requirements maintain an aircrew member at 85% MRP per T&R Program Manual.

161. SYLLABUS MATRICES. These matrices display specific event information such as; flight/simulator hours, refly interval, prerequisites, CRP, chaining, etc.

HH-46D/E SAR PILOT													
CORE SKILL BASIC (200 SERIES)													
STAGE	TRNG CODE	FLT HOURS	SIM HOURS	REFLY INTERVAL	POI	EVAL	TOTAL A/C	TYPE	CONDITIONS	PREQ	EVENT DESC	CRP	CHAINING	EVENT CONV
OFT														
OFT	200		1.0	*	SC,R	X		S			HH-46 INTRO	0.25		100
OFT	201		1.0	*	R			S			DOPPLER INTRO	0.25		102
OFT	202		1.0	*	SC,R			S			DOPPLER & EP	0.25		103, 106
		0.0	3.0									0.75		
FAM/EP														
FAM	203	1.5		*	R		1	A			AREA FAM	0.25		108
FAM	204	1.5		*	SC,R		1	A			EP FAM "E"	0.50		109
FAM	205	1.5		*	R		1	A			EP FAM "D"	0.50		
		4.5	0.0									1.25		
INST														
INST	210	1.5		*	SC,R		1	A	(N)		REV BI & RI "E"	0.50		110
INST	211	1.5		*	R		1	A	(N)		REV BI & RI "D"	0.50		
INST	212	1.5		*	R		1	A	(N)		PRACTICE BI & RI	0.50		
		4.5	0.0									1.50		
CAL														
CAL	220	1.5		*	R		1	A			DAY CAL	0.50		120
		1.5	0.0									0.50		
FF														
FF	240	1.5		*	R		1	A			BAMBI BUCKET	1.00		140
		1.5	0.0									1.00		
SAR														
SAR	250	1.5	0.0	365	SC,R		1	A		203,204,205, 220	INTRO GPS "E"	1.00		200
SAR	251	1.5	0.0	365	R		1	A		203,204,205, 220	INTRO GPS "D"	1.00		
SAR	252	1.5	0.0	365	R		1	A		203,204,205, 220	DAY SEARCH	1.00	251,250	202
SAR	253	1.5	0.0	365	R		1	A		203,204,205, 220	DAY LAND HOIST	1.00		203
SAR	254	1.5	0.0	365	R		1	A		253	DAY RAMP HOIST	1.00		204
SAR	255	2.0	0.0	365	R		1	A		250,251,252, 253	DAY SAREX	1.00	253,252, 251,250, 220	205
SAR	256	1.5	0.0	365	SC,R		1	A		203,204,205, 220	DAY DOPPLER "E"	1.00	250	
SAR	257	1.5	0.0	365	R		1	A		203,204,205, 220	DAY DOPPLER "D"	1.00	251	206
SAR	258	1.5	0.0	365	R		1	A		253,256,257	DAY WATER WORKS	1.00	257,256, 251,250	207
SAR	260	1.5	0.0	365	R		1	A		253,256,257, 258	DAY BOAT HOIST	1.00	258,257, 256,251, 250	209
		15.5	0.0									10.00		
PHASE TOTAL														
FLT HRS	27.5	3.0	SIM HRS									15.00	CRP TOTAL	

STAGE	TRNG CODE	FLT HOURS	SIM HOURS	REFLY INTERVAL	POI	EVAL	TOTAL A/C	TYPE	CONDITIONS	PREQ	EVENT DESC	CRP	CHAINING	EVENT CONV
								HH-46D/E SAR PILOT						
								CORE SKILL ADVANCED (300 SERIES)						
								NVG						
NVG	300	1.5		365	R		1	A	NS	203,204,205 210,211,220	NVG HLL FAM	1.0	251,250	300
NVG	301	1.5		365	R		1	A	NS	300	NVG CALS	1.5	300,251,250,220	301
NVG	302	1.5		365	R		1	A	NS	300	NVG NAV	1.5	300,251,250	302
		4.5	0.0									4.0		
								NSAR						
NSAR	320	1.5		365	R		1	A	N	302,252	NIGHT LAND SEARCH	2.0	302,300,252,251, 250	321
NSAR	321	1.5		365	R		1	A	N	302,253	NIGHT LAND HOIST	2.0	302,300,253,251, 250	322
NSAR	322	2.0		365	R		1	A	N	302,255,320 321	NIGHT LAND SAREX	2.0	321,320,302,301 300,255,253,252 251,250,220	323
NSAR	323	1.5		365	SC R		1	A	N	302,256	NIGHT DOPPLER "E"	2.0	320,302,300,257, 256,252,251,250	
NSAR	324	1.5		365	R		1	A	N	302,257	NIGHT DOPPLER "D"	2.0	320,302,300,257, 256,252,251,250	324
NSAR	330	1.5		365	R		1	A	N	258,302,320 321,323,324	NIGHT WATER WORKS	2.0	324,323,302,300 258,257,256,252, 251,250	325
NSAR	333	1.5		365	R		1	A	N	260,302,330	NIGHT BOAT HOIST	2.0	330,324,323,302 300,260,258,257, 256,251,250	327
NSAR	340	2.0		365	R		1	A	N	302,333	NIGHT WATER SAREX	2.0	320,302,300,252, 251,250	328
		13.0	0.0									16		
								PHASE TOTAL						
FLT HRS		4.5	0.0	SIM HRS								20	CRP TOTAL	

STAGE	TRNG CODE	FLT HOURS	SIM HOURS	REFLY INTERVAL	POI	EVAL	TOTAL A/C	TYPE	CONDITIONS	PREQ	EVENT DESC	CRP	CHAINING	EVENT CONV
CORE PLUS (400 SERIES)														
RAP														
RAP	402	1.5		365	R		1	A		220,253	SAR RAPPEL	1.0	251,250, 220	402
		0.0	0.0									1.0		
FCLP														
FCLP	410	1.5		365	R		1	A			DAY FCLP	1.0		410
FCLP	411	1.5		365	R		1	A	NS	410	NIGHT FCLP	1.0	410	411
		3.0	0.0									2.0		
CQ														
CQ	420	1.5		365	R		1	A		410	DAY CQ	1.0	410	420
CQ	421	1.5		365	R		1	A	NS	411,420	NIGHT CQ	1.0	420,411 410	421
		3.0	0.0									2.0		
PHASE TOTAL														
FLT HRS		6.0	0.0	SIM HRS								5.0	CRP TOTAL	

										HH-46D/E SAR PILOT			
									INSTRUCTOR TRAINING (500 SERIES)				
STAGE	TRNG CODE	FLT HOURS	SIM HOURS	REFLY INTERVAL	POI	EVAL	TOTAL A/C	TYPE	CONDITIONS	PREQ	EVENT DESC	CRP	CHAINING	EVENT CONV
									IUT					
IUT	500	1.5		*		X	1	A			IUT DAY FAM/CAL/EP	0.00		500
IUT	503	1.5		*		X	1	A			IUT DAY WATER BUCKET	0.00		502
IUT	504	3.0		*		X	1	A	(N)	500,503	IUT SAR CHECK	0.00		503
		0.0	0.0									0.00		
									NSSI					
NSSI	550	2.0		*		X	1	A	NS		NSSI FAM	0.00		
NSSI	551	2.0		*		X	1	A	NS		NSSI NAV	0.00		
NSSI	552	2.0		*		X	1	A	NS	550,551	NSSI SAR & EVAL	0.00		
		6.0	0.0									0.00		
									PHASE TOTAL					
FLT HRS		6.0	0.0	SIM HRS								0.00	CRP TOTAL	
								REQUIREMENTS, QUALIFICATIONS, & DESIGNATIONS [RQD] (600 SERIES)					
STAGE	TRNG CODE	FLT HOURS	SIM HOURS	REFLY INTERVAL	POI	EVAL	TOTAL A/C	TYPE	CONDITIONS	PREQ	EVENT DESC	CRP	CHAINING	EVENT CONV
									RQD					
RQD	600	1.5		365		X	1	A	(N)		NATOPS EVAL	0.00		600
RQD	601	1.5		365		X	1	A	(N)		INST EVAL	0.00		601
RQD	602	3.0		365		X	1	A			DAY SAR EVAL	0.00		602
RQD	603	3.0		365		X	1	A	N		NIGHT SAR EVAL	0.00		603
RQD	604	1.5		*		X	1	A			FCF EVAL	0.00		604
RQD	640	1.5		365		X	1	A	(N)		ANNUAL CRM EVAL	0.00		640
		12.0	0.0									0.00		
									PHASE TOTAL					
FLT HRS		12.0	0.0	SIM HRS								0.00	CRP TOTAL	

SYLLABUS EVENT CONVERSION MATRIX

OLD STAGE	OLD TRNG CODE	NEW STAGE	NEW TRNG CODE
		200 LEVEL	
OFT	100	OFT	200
	101		
	102		201
	103		202
	104		
	105		
	106		202
FAM	108	FAM	203
	109	EP "E"	204
		EP "D"	205
INST	110	INST "E"	210
		INST "D"	211
		INST "D"	212
CAL	120	CAL	220
FF	140	FF	240

OLD STAGE	OLD TRNG CODE	NEW STAGE	NEW TRNG CODE
		200 LEVEL	
SAR	200	SAR "E"	250
		SAR "D"	251
	202		252
	203		253
	204		254
	205		255
			256
	206		257
	207		258
	209		260

Figure 1-1.--Pilot Syllabus Conversion Matrix.

SYLLABUS EVENT CONVERSION MATRIX

OLD STAGE	OLD TRNG CODE	NEW STAGE	NEW TRNG CODE
	300 LEVEL		
NVG	300	NVG	300
	301		301
	302		302
	303		
NSAR	321	NSAR	320
	322		321
	323		322
			323
	324		324
	325		330
	327		333
	328		340

OLD STAGE	OLD TRNG CODE	NEW STAGE	NEW TRNG CODE
	400 LEVEL		
RAP	402	RAP	402
FCLP	410	FCLP	410
	411		411
CQ	420	CQ	420
	421		421

Figure 1-1.--Pilot Syllabus Conversion Matrix—Continued.

SYLLABUS EVENT CONVERSION MATRIX

OLD STAGE	OLD TRNG CODE	NEW STAGE	NEW TRNG CODE
	500 LEVEL		
FAM	500	FAM	500
FF	502	FF	503
SAR	503	SAR	504
		NVD	550
			551
			552

OLD STAGE	OLD TRNG CODE	NEW STAGE	NEW TRNG CODE
	600 LEVEL		
RQD	600	RQD	600
	601		601
	602		602
	603		603
	604		604
	640		640

Figure 1-1.--Pilot Syllabus Conversion Matrix—Continued.

Aviation Training Form

Instructor	Date	NVG Time				
Location	Flight Time	Doppler				
			DM	DC	NM	NC

ALL FLIGHTS:

Preparation	U	BA	A	AA	NA
Load Computation	U	BA	A	AA	NA
T&R Requirements	U	BA	A	AA	NA
Aircrew Brief	U	BA	A	AA	NA
Systems Knowledge	U	BA	A	AA	NA
Emergency Procedures	U	BA	A	AA	NA
Taxi	U	BA	A	AA	NA
Basic Air Work	U	BA	A	AA	NA
Headwork	U	BA	A	AA	NA
Course Rules	U	BA	A	AA	NA
SOP Items	U	BA	A	AA	NA

FAMILIARIZATION:

Minimum Power Take Off	U	BA	A	AA	NA
Obstacle Take Off	U	BA	A	AA	NA
Running Take Off	U	BA	A	AA	NA
Vertical Take Off	U	BA	A	AA	NA
Precision Approach	U	BA	A	AA	NA
Normal Approach	U	BA	A	AA	NA
Autorotation	U	BA	A	AA	NA
Quick Stop	U	BA	A	AA	NA
AFCS Off Flight	U	BA	A	AA	NA
No Hover Landing	U	BA	A	AA	NA

NAVIGATION:

Map Study	U	BA	A	AA	NA
Terrain Association	U	BA	A	AA	NA
Dead Reckoning	U	BA	A	AA	NA
Proper Use of Nav Equip	U	BA	A	AA	NA

CONFINED AREA LANDINGS:

Approach	U	BA	A	AA	NA
Power Control	U	BA	A	AA	NA
Airspeed Control	U	BA	A	AA	NA
Cross Wind Take Off / Landing	U	BA	A	AA	NA

SAR Evolutions:

Headwork	U	BA	A	AA	NA
Transition To a Hover	U	BA	A	AA	NA
Control Over Survivor	U	BA	A	AA	NA
Pickup	U	BA	A	AA	NA

EXTERNAL LOADS:

Headwork	U	BA	A	AA	NA
Pattern	U	BA	A	AA	NA
Approach	U	BA	A	AA	NA
Transition To a Hover	U	BA	A	AA	NA
Control Over Load	U	BA	A	AA	NA
Hook Up	U	BA	A	AA	NA
Transition To Forward Flight	U	BA	A	AA	NA

NIGHT VISION GOGGLES:

Taxi					
Hover Work	U	BA	A	AA	NA
Vertical Take Off	U	BA	A	AA	NA
Vertical Landing	U	BA	A	AA	NA
No Hover Landing	U	BA	A	AA	NA
Precision Approach	U	BA	A	AA	NA
Pattern Work	U	BA	A	AA	NA

CARRIER QUALIFICATION:

Pattern	U	BA	A	AA	NA
Approach	U	BA	A	AA	NA
Take Off	U	BA	A	AA	NA
Landing	U	BA	A	AA	NA
Voice Procedures	U	BA	A	AA	NA

CREW RESOURCE MANAGEMENT

Decision Making	U	BA	A	AA	NA
Assertiveness	U	BA	A	AA	NA
Mission Analysis	U	BA	A	AA	NA
Communication	U	BA	A	AA	NA
Leadership	U	BA	A	AA	NA
Adaptability / Flexibility	U	BA	A	AA	NA
Situational Awareness	U	BA	A	AA	NA

Comments:

PUI: Training Code:

Figure 1-2.--Aircrew Training Form.

CHAPTER 2

HH-46D/E (SAR) CREW CHIEF

FIGURE

* * **N O T E** * *

Aircrews shall include Crew Resource Management techniques as part of their brief.

CHAPTER 2

HH-46D/E (SAR) CREW CHIEF

200. <u>MARINE SEARCH AND RESCUE UNIT - HH-46D/E</u>

1. <u>General</u>. The capabilities defined and described in the core capability and unit template sections are provided to ensure each like-SAR unit maintains a common base of training and depth of capabilities. When sources permit and when, in the judgment of the commander, additional training would significantly increase the unit's Search and Rescue capability, training to a level above these base capabilities is permitted. It is incumbent upon and expected of commanders to balance any increase in the depth of core capabilities against the long-term health and readiness of their unit while staying within resource constraints.

2. <u>Mission</u>. To provide heliborne SAR capabilities to tenant aviation units. Additional missions are secondary in nature and shall be accepted on a not-to-interfere basis only.

3. <u>Mission Essential Task List (METL)</u>

   a. Provide Search and Rescue for tenant aircraft.

   b. Provide supplemental Search and Rescue asset for U. S. Coast Guard and U.S. Air Force.

   c. Provide MEDEVAC capability to local civilian agencies as required, on a not-to-interfere basis.

   d. Provide airborne fire-fighting capability for MCAS facilities and to supplement local area Forest Service assets.

   e. Provide supplemental Search and Rescue to local civilian agencies for non-law enforcement type missions such as searches, fire fighting, disaster response, or civilian MEDEVAC, when civilian agencies cannot respond.

   f. Provide utility and logistical support missions for MCAS activities as directed by the Director of Operations, Marine Corps Installations (MCI) EAST.

   g. Enhance public relations for the Commanding General, MCI EAST through static displays and flight demonstrations as authorized by higher authority.

4. <u>Table of Organization</u>

                    3 HH-46D/E helicopters
                    8 Pilots
                    9 Crew Chiefs
                    6 SAR Swimmers
                    4 SAR Medical Technicians

5. <u>Squadron Core Capability</u>

   a. A core capable squadron is able to sustain the following minimum performance on a daily basis during sustained search and rescue operations, assuming at least 100% Primary Authorized Allowance (PAA), 90% in reporting

status, and 90% T/O on hand in all MOSs. If <90%, core capability will be
degraded by like-percentage. The extent to which a core capable squadron is
able to surge beyond its core capability is situational dependent.

    b. A core capable squadron is able to launch 1 full mission capable
aircraft crewed by a fully qualified aircrew at all times. This aircraft
must be airborne within 15 minutes of alert when operating under SAR
Condition I and 1 hour under SAR Condition II.

201. <u>PROGRAMS OF INSTRUCTION (POI)</u>

1. All HH-46D/E SAR Crew Chiefs are required to obtain basic Air
Crewman Training at Pensacola, Fl. and be designated a CH-46E Crew Chief by
HMMT-164 at Camp Pendleton, Ca. prior to undergoing Basic SAR training in
either the HH-46D and/or HH-46E.

2. The BASIC POI is for all CH-46E Crew Chiefs who are making a conversion
to the HH-46D/E for the purpose of SAR and all refresher Crew Chiefs who have
previously flown SAR in the HH-46D/E. The Basic POI includes all 200 - 400
events.

3. The Series Conversion POI is for SAR qualified Crew Chiefs current in
the HH-46D who are making a conversion the HH-46E.

202. <u>SQUADRON LEVEL TRAINING</u>

    NATOPS Flight Manual and NATOPS Pocket Checklist
    Search and Rescue (SAR) Publications
    Safety Publications
    Squadron Standard Operating Procedures (SOPs)
    Inspection, Utilization, and Limitations of Personal Aviation Survival
    Equipment
    Inspection, Utilization, and Limitations of SAR Equipment
    Hand and Arm Signals
    CPR Certification
    First Aid Training
    Search and Rescue Techniques
    Fire Bucket (Bambi Bucket) Operations Manual
    Night Vision Device Ground Training
    Ordnance Safety
    HIRA Ground Syllabus
    FCF Syllabus

203. <u>FLIGHT TRAINING FOR BASIC AND REFRESHER CREW CHIEFS</u>. Basic and
Refresher Crew Chiefs in model H-46 helicopter will be programmed to fly the
complete program of instruction, regardless of qualifications. All initial
flights shall be flown with a designated NATOPS Instructor.

204. <u>FLIGHT TRAINING FOR SERIES CONVERSION (SC) CREW CHIEFS</u>

1. Crew Chiefs who are current in model HH-46D will be programmed to fly the
SC syllabus. The SC syllabus is far more intensive for the pilots than Crew
Chiefs and as a result there are only two flights in the SC syllabus.

2. Core Skill Introduction, NVG Core Skill Advanced, and Core Skill Plus
qualifications that are current per this Manual and the CH-46E T&R Manual

remain current upon transfer to the HH-46D, upon approval of the SAR unit commanding officer.

205. REQUIREMENTS FOR SAR CREW CHIEF DESIGNATION

1. Complete the CD Rom based SAR academic lectures.

2. Complete SAR Open Book Examination, NATOPS Open and Closed Book Examination.

3. T&R Codes complete through 340. Personnel may be designated as Day SAR Crew Chief at the discretion of the Commanding Officer once SAR T&R codes complete through SAR 260. Personnel may be designated as HH-46D/E non-SAR Crew Chief once complete with T&R FF-240 and a current NATOPS and CRM Evaluation.

4. NATOPS Evaluation, SAR Crew Chief Evaluation and CRM Evaluation (T&R Codes 600, 602 and 640).

206. FLIGHT TRAINING FOR BASIC AND REFRESHER CREW CHIEFS. All initial syllabus flights shall be flown with a designated NATOPS Instructor or Assistant NATOPS Instructor.

207. FLIGHT TRAINING FOR SERIES CONVERSION

1. Core Skill Basic, NVG Core Skill Advanced, and Core Skill Plus qualifications per this Manual and the CH-46E T&R Manual remain current upon transfer to the HH-46D/E, pending approval of the SAR unit commanding officer.

220. GROUND/ACADEMIC TRAINING COURSES OF INSTRUCTION

COURSE/PHASE	ACTIVITY
Naval Aircrew Candidate School	NAS Pensacola
Rappel Indoctrination Course*	HC-3

*Completion of the Rappel Indoctrination Course is highly recommended but not required.

230. FLIGHT PERFORMANCE REQUIREMENTS

1. Purpose. Promote standardization of the Crew Chief procedures and develop proficiency in servicing, loading, in-flight procedures. To establish minimum training requirements for personnel assigned as a Crew Chief aboard the HH-46D/E.

2. General

    a. Personnel shall complete the Naval Air Crewman Candidate School.

    b. Crew chiefs who are current in model HH-46D will be programmed to fly the SC syllabus. All other crew chiefs will be programmed to fly the complete POI regardless of qualifications.

    c. All initial flights shall be flown with a designated NATOPS/Assistant NATOPS Instructor.

   d. Local commands are granted the authority to waive requirements that are not applicable to the local operating environment.

   e. All flights shall terminate with a comprehensive debrief with emphasis on the aircrew's performance using all evaluation techniques.

   f. Aircrews shall fly events annotated with an N at least 30 minutes after official sunset. Aircrews may fly events annotated with (N) at night.

   g. Aircrews shall fly events annotated with an NS with Night Vision Devices (NVDs) for the entire flight. Aircrews may fly events with (NS) with the option of using NVDs.

   h. All flights annotated with an E shall be evaluated per T&R Program Manual.

   i. Environmental conditions (day or night) or Night Systems conditions shall be annotated in flight events and the syllabus matrix as follows:

Code	Requirement
D	Shall be flown or conducted during day.
N	Shall be flown or conducted at night (using available night vision devices or flown unaided).
(N)	May be flown or conducted day or night; if at night, available night vision devices may be used or flown unaided.
NS	Shall be flown or conducted at night using available night vision devices.
(NS)	May be flown or conducted day or night; if at night, available night vision devices shall be used.
N*	Event Shall be flown or conducted at night unaided.
(N*)	Event may be flown or conducted at night; if at night, shall be flown unaided.

3. Re-fly Interval. The syllabus matrix shows re-fly interval and Mission Readiness Percentage for MOS 6172.

4. Aircrew Evaluation Flights. All crew chiefs are required to complete a NATOPS evaluation form annually upon completion of the following:

   a. NATOPS Evaluation flights (RQD-600).

   b. Search and Rescue/NATOPS Evaluation flights (RQD-602).

   c. Crew Resource Management Evaluation (RQD-640).

5. Crew Resource Management (CRM). Aircrews shall include CRM techniques as part of their brief.

231. CORE SKILL BASIC TRAINING

1. Familiarization

    a. Purpose. Familiarize the trainee with HH-46 operations and procedures.

    b. General. These flights may be flown on any appropriate flight of the pilot syllabus.

    c. Crew Requirement. CCI/CCUI.

    d. Flight Training (3 flights, 4.5 hours)

FAM-203   1.5   R   1 HH-46D/E

    Goal. Conduct an area and aircraft familiarization. Introduce HH-46 emergency procedures and characteristics. Discuss CRM.

    Requirements. The CCUI will act in the capacity of the crew chief. The CC will instruct the CCUI in the duties of the crew chief, to include Look-out Doctrine, Daily Inspection, and Turn-Around procedures. The trainee should accompany the crew chief during the Daily and Turn-Around inspections.

    Performance Standard. CCUI shall be able to identify differences between HH-46D and CH-46E series helicopters, and perform familiarization maneuvers per NATOPS Manual.

EP-204   1.5   SC,R   1 HH-46E

    Goal. Conduct Emergency Procedures familiarization and review area familiarization.

    Requirements. The CCUI will act in the capacity of the crew chief. The CC will discuss emergency procedures in-depth, to include engine fire in-flight, engine fire on ground, fuselage fire in-flight, fuselage fire on ground, emergency landings (land and water), and smoke and fume elimination.

    Performance Standard. CCUI shall demonstrate knowledge of aircraft systems, perform basic FAM maneuvers, and be able to satisfactorily perform emergency procedures per NATOPS manual.

EP-205   1.5   R   1 HH-46D

    Goal. Conduct Emergency Procedures familiarization and review area familiarization.

    Requirements. The CCUI will act in the capacity of the crew chief. The CC will discuss emergency procedures in-depth, to include engine fire in-flight, engine fire on ground, fuselage fire in-flight, fuselage fire on ground, emergency landings (land and water), and smoke and fume elimination.

Performance Standard. CCUI shall demonstrate knowledge of aircraft systems, perform basic FAM maneuvers, and be able to satisfactorily perform emergency procedures per NATOPS manual.

CAL-220   1.5   R   1 HH-46D/E

Goal. Conduct Day Confined Area Landings.

Requirements. The CCUI will act in the capacity of the crew chief. The CCUI will develop and demonstrate proficiency in the crew coordination requirements of Confined Area Operations. Emphasize aircraft, terrain, and obstacle clearance during take-off and landing.

Performance Standard. CCUI will demonstrate the ability to successfully crew the aircraft to the deck for a minimum of 5 landings.

2. Internal Loads

    a. Purpose. Introduce procedures for the loading, securing, and transportation of internal cargo and personnel. Introduce procedures for the loading, servicing, and operation of the internal Extended Range Fuel Tank.

    b. General. These flights may be flown with any flight where internal cargo, passengers, and Extended Range Fuel Tanks are carried and/or utilized.

    c. Crew Requirement. CCI/CCUI.

    d. Flight Training (1 flight, 1.5 hours)

INT-230   1.5   SC,R   1 HH-46E

Goal. Review procedures for internal cargo loading, security, and unloading. Review procedures for passenger embarkation, debarkation, briefing and safety procedures.

Requirement. CCUI will act in the capacity of the crew chief. CCUI will observe and assist in the proper handling of internal cargo and passengers. CCUI will demonstrate the proper procedures for servicing and operation of the Range Extension Fuel Tank. Review emergency landing/ditching procedures.

Performance Standard. CCUI will demonstrate the ability to safely embark and debark passengers, litter patients, and cargo. CCUI will demonstrate the ability to safely refuel and manage in-flight responsibilities for the internal fuel tank.

INT-231   1.5   R   1 HH-46D

Goal. Review procedures for internal cargo loading, security, and unloading. Review procedures for passenger embarkation, debarkation, briefing and safety procedures.

Requirement. CCUI will act in the capacity of the crew chief. CCUI will observe and assist in the proper handling of internal cargo and passengers. CCUI will demonstrate the proper procedures for servicing and operation of the Range Extension Fuel Tank. Review emergency landing/ditching procedures.

Performance Standard. CCUI will demonstrate the ability to safely embark and debark passengers, litter patients, and cargo. CCUI will demonstrate the ability to safely refuel and manage in-flight responsibilities for the internal fuel tank.

3. Fire Fighting

    a. Purpose. Develop the ability to conduct water bucket operations.

    b. General. These flights may be flown in conjunction with fire fighting flights in the pilot syllabus.

    c. Crew Requirement. CCI/ CCUI.

    d. Flight Training (1 flight, 1.5 hours)

FF-240   1.5   R   1 HH-46D/E

        Goal. Review cargo hook and Bambi Bucket hook-up procedures, verbal commands and communication, and water bucket operations. Review emergency external disconnect procedures.

        Requirement. CCUI will act in the capacity of the crew chief. CCUI will assist the crew chief in external load operations. Instruct CCUI in water bucket operations, verbal communication, emergency disconnect procedures, and review static discharge precautions.

        Performance Standard. CCUI shall be able to safely fill Bambi Bucket, complete minimum of 5 hookups and water drops, and deliver water to fire within 5 meters of intended point of impact.

4. Day Search and Rescue

    a. Purpose. Develop proficiency in Day Search and Rescue operations to include in-flight procedures, SAR equipment, search patterns and techniques, Doppler approach procedures, over land and over water rescue/recovery techniques, and safety regulations.

    b. General

        (1) The T&R Program Manual addresses the commanding officer's authority to modify this training as required. Personnel will complete the appropriate NAMTRAGRUDET and NATOPS ground school syllabus prior to commencing the flight training syllabus. A NATOPS Instructor will monitor the trainee's progress during the flight training syllabus.

        (2) Local commands are granted the authority to designate crew chiefs in model HH-46 upon completion of the flights listed in paragraph 242.1.c.\

   c. <u>Prerequisite</u>

      (1) The HH-46 crew chief syllabus shall be satisfactorily completed by Basic and Refresher crew chiefs not current in model H-46 prior to commencing the SAR qualification training phase.

      (2) Crew Chiefs may be designated as HH-46D/E (non-SAR) Crew Chiefs at the discretion of the unit commanding officer prior to completion of the day and/or night SAR syllabi. Crew Chiefs who have not completed the appropriate SAR syllabus shall not be assigned to SAR duty (day or night) until completion of the appropriate syllabus. Local commands are granted the authority to designate personnel as Day SAR Crew Chief qualified upon completion of the Day Search and Rescue syllabus (see paragraph 205).

      (3) The following flights of the Core Skill Basic phase shall be satisfactorily completed prior to commencement of Day SAR Core Skills Basic qualification training:

           (1) FAM-203

           (2) EP-204/205

           (3) CAL-220

           (4) INT-231

   d. <u>Ground Training</u>. Additional ground training requirements for all SAR crew chiefs are as follows:

      (1) Utilization and limitations of SAR equipment.

      (2) Search and Rescue techniques.

      (3) Ground-to-air signals to include body, panel, lighting signals, and international ground-to-air emergency codes.

   e. <u>Crew Requirement</u>. CCI/CCUI.

   f. <u>Flight Training (9 flights, 14 hours)</u>

SAR-250   <u>1.5</u>   <u>R</u>   <u>1 HH-46D/E</u>

       <u>Goal</u>. Introduction to GPS and dead reckoning navigation.

       <u>Requirement</u>. Assist the pilot with map and GPS navigation by identifying direction and key terrain features. Review "away from base" re-fueling and supply requisitioning procedures. Assist the pilot in various search patterns by providing appropriate lookout doctrine.

       <u>Performance Standard</u>. CCUI shall safely assist the pilots in navigation utilizing the GPS and a map for dead reckoning.

SAR-252   <u>1.5</u>   <u>R</u>   <u>1 HH-46D/E</u>

       <u>Goal</u>. Conduct search patterns and overland search procedures.

Requirement. CCI will introduce day SAR procedures and review standard ICS voice communications, introduce and demonstrate the crew chief's Remote Hover Coupler Station, and discuss vertigo. The CCUI, acting in the capacity of crew chief, will demonstrate crew chief duties during day, overland search operations, day manual and coupled Doppler approaches. The CCUI will complete a minimum of 2 day manual and 2 day coupled approaches.

Performance Standard. CCUI shall assist the pilots in conducting a search pattern consisting of a minimum of 5 checkpoints, and maintain within 500 meters of course line. CCUI shall provide calls to the pilot to conduct a hover for crewmember deployment, maintaining within 5 feet of hover point.

SAR-253   1.5   R   1 HH-46D/E

Goal. Conduct day overland hoisting operations utilizing the Rescue Strop, Forest Penetrator, Rescue Litter, MEDEVAC Litter, Rescue Net, and Hoisting Vest (if available).

Requirement. The CCI will introduce overland hoist procedures per NWP-3-50, utilization of SAR equipment, introduce use of Quick Splice and Chicago Grip. The CCUI, acting in the capacity of crew chief, will demonstrate the deployment and recovery of the Rescue Strop, Forest Penetrator, Rescue Litter, MEDEVAC Litter, Rescue Net, and Hoisting Vest in a confined area. Demonstrate the use of the Quick Splice and Chicago Grip. Review standard ICS voice communications and safety procedures. Review hand, arm, and Aldis Lamp signals.

Performance Standard. CCUI shall provide calls to the pilot to conduct a hover for crewmember deployment, maintaining within 5 feet of hover point. The CCUI will safely conduct hoisting operations utilizing the Rescue Strop, Forest Penetrator, Rescue Litter, MEDEVAC Litter, Rescue Net, and Hoisting Vest.

SAR-254   1.5   R   1 HH-46D/E

Goal. Conduct day hoisting operations with rescue devices utilizing the internal winch through the cabin floor rescue hatch and/or aft cargo hatch.

Requirement. The CCUI, acting in the capacity of crew chief, will demonstrate hoisting operations with rescue devices utilizing the cabin floor rescue hatch and aft cargo hatch in a confined area. Review over-land SAR procedures per NWP-3-50. Review standard ICS voice communications and safety procedures. Review hand, arm, and Aldis Lamp signals.

Performance Standard. CCUI shall provide calls to the pilot to conduct a hover for crewmember deployment, maintaining within 5 feet of hover point. The CCUI will safely conduct hoisting operations utilizing the Rescue Strop, Forest Penetrator, Rescue Litter, MEDEVAC Litter, Rescue Net, and Hoisting Vest.

Prerequisite. SAR-253.

SAR-255   2.0   R   1 HH-46D/E

Goal. Conduct day, overland SAREX. Assist the pilots with navigation and search. Prepare the aircraft for accepting patients and/or survivors. Assist the SARRACs with transporting patient/survivor to helicopter.

Requirement. CCUI will act in the capacity of the crew chief. CCUI will demonstrate overland SAR procedures per NWP-3-50. Demonstrate the deployment and recovery of rescue devices. Demonstrate standard ICS voice communications and safety procedures. Demonstrate hand, arm, and Aldis Lamp signals.

Performance Standard. CCUI shall assist the pilots in navigation, provide calls to the pilot to conduct a hover for crewmember deployment maintaining within 5 feet of hover point. The CCUI will safely conduct hoisting operations, assist the SARRACs with patient transport to helicopter and secure patient into litter stanchions as required.

Prerequisite. SAR-250, SAR-252, SAR-253.

SAR-256   1.5   R   1 HH-46D/E

Goal. Conduct day over water search and Doppler approaches.

Requirement. CCUI will act in the capacity of the crew chief. CCUI will demonstrate the duties of the crew chief during day, manual and coupled over water Doppler approaches. Review standard ICS voice communications. CCI will introduce and discuss flare deployment and vertigo. Introduce and demonstrate the Remote Hover Coupler Station. CCUI will complete a minimum of 2 day manual and 2 day coupled approaches.

Performance Standard. CCUI shall provide calls to the pilot to conduct a hover for crewmember deployment, maintaining within 5 feet of hover point. The CCUI will safely conduct hoisting operations utilizing the Rescue Strop, Rescue Litter, MEDEVAC Litter, and Rescue Net. CCUI will maintain a hover utilizing the Remote Hover Coupler Station, and maintain within 5 feet of hover point.

SAR-258   1.5   R   1 HH-46D/E

Goal. Conduct day rescue swimmer deployments and recoveries with rescue strop and net.

Requirement. CCUI will act in the capacity of the crew chief. Review deployment and recovery procedures of rescue swimmer per NWP-3-50 and local SOP. Deploy and recover the rescue swimmer and simulated survivor(s) utilizing the Rescue Strop and Rescue Net. Conduct a minimum of 1 short haul. Review flare deployment and safety, standard ICS voice communications, hand, arm, and Aldis Lamp signals, and operation of the crew chief Remote Hover Coupler Station.

Performance Standard. CCUI shall provide calls to the pilot to
conduct a hover for crewmember deployment, maintaining within 5
feet of hover point. The CCUI will safely conduct hoisting
operations utilizing the Rescue Strop, Rescue Seat, and Rescue
Net. CCUI will conduct 2 hovers utilizing the Remote Hover
Coupler Station, and maintain hover within 5 feet of intended
hover point.

Prerequisite. SAR-253, SAR-256.

Ordnance. 1 Mk-25 Flare, 1 Mk-58 Flare.

SAR-259   1.5   R   1 HH-46D/E

Goal. Conduct day rescue swimmer deployments and recoveries with
stokes and SAR litters.

Requirement. CCUI will act in the capacity of the crew chief.
Review deployment and recovery procedures of rescue swimmer per
NWP-3-50 and local SOP. Deploy and recover the rescue swimmer
and simulated survivor(s) utilizing the stokes nad SAR litters.
Demonstrate proper utilization of the Trail Line assembly.
Review standard ICS voice communication and safety procedures.
Review hand, arm, and Aldis Lamp signals. Review operation of
the Remote Hover Coupler Station. Review flare deployment and
safety.

Performance Standard. CCUI shall provide calls to the pilot to
conduct a hover for crewmember deployment, maintaining within 5
feet of hover point. The CCUI will safely conduct hoisting
operations utilizing the Rescue litter, and MEDEVAC litter. CCUI
will conduct 2 hovers utilizing the Remote Hover Coupler Station,
and maintain hover within 5 feet of intended hover point.

Prerequisite. SAR-258.

Ordnance. 1 Mk-25 Flare, 1 Mk 58 Flare.

SAR-260   1.5   R   1 HH-46D/E

Goal. Conduct day SAR boat hoist.

Requirement. CCUI will act in the capacity of the crew chief.
Conduct hoisting operations from a boat or ship with emphasis on
the SAR litter, strop, and trail line assembly. Discuss normal
and emergency procedures related to shipboard hoisting
operations. Emphasize Crew Coordination and Situational
Awareness as part of CRM brief. Review standard ICS voice
communications and safety procedures. Review hand, arm, and
Aldis Lamp signals.

Performance Standard. CCUI shall provide calls to the pilot to
conduct a hover over a boat for crewmember deployment,
maintaining within 5 feet of hover point. The CCUI will safely
conduct hoisting operations utilizing the SAR litter, stokes, and
trail line assembly.

Prerequisite. SAR-253, SAR-256, SAR-258.

232. CORE SKILL ADVANCED TRAINING

1. Night Vision Goggle (NVG) Operations

a. Purpose. Develop proficiency required to safely conduct basic operations, navigation, and search patterns utilizing NVGs.

b. Search and Rescue NSQ consists of NVG-300 through SAR-340.

c. Safety. Rappels and short-hauls shall not be conducted while using NVGs.

d. Prerequisites. The completion of the NVG Night Lab and the following flights are required prior to commencing the NVG syllabus:

(1) FAM-203

(2) EP-204, 205

(3) CAL-220

e. Crew Requirement. CCNSSI/CCUI.

f. Flight Training (4 flights, 6.0 hours)

NVG-300   1.5   R   1 HH-46D/E   NS

Goal. NVG familiarization flight in HLL conditions.

Requirement

(1) Introduce wear and use of NVGs during low work and touch and go landings.

(2) Brief/Discuss

(a) Use and limitations of NVGs.

(b) NVG tube and battery failures.

(c) Lookout Doctrine.

(d) NVG scan patterns.

(e) Obstacle clearance.

(f) Emergency procedures.

Performance Standard. CCUI shall be able to safely perform familiarization maneuvers while on NVGs per NFM, and MAWTS-1 NVG Manual.

NVG-301   1.5   R   1 HH-46D/E   NS

Goal. Develop proficiency in conducting confined area landings while utilizing NVGs. This fight may be conducted in HLL or LLL.

Requirement

(1) Introduce confined area landings.

(2) Brief/discuss

    (a) Obstacle clearance.

    (b) Terrain suitability.

    (c) Rate of closure.

    (d) Loss of depth perception.

    (e) Lookout Doctrine.

    (f) NVG scan techniques.

    (g) Vertigo.

    (h) Emergency procedures.

Performance Standard. CCUI will demonstrate the ability to successfully crew the aircraft to the deck for a minimum of 5 landings while wearing NVGs.

Prerequisite. NVG-300.

NVG-302   1.5   R   1 HH-46D/E   NS

Goal. Develop proficiency in low level navigation with NVGs. This flight may be conducted in HLL or LLL.

Requirement. Conduct low level navigation with NVGs. Introduce operation and limitations of the Night Sun searchlight.

Brief /Discuss

(a) Lookout Doctrine.

(b) NVG scan techniques.

(c) Night Sun search light and its effects on NVGs.

(d) Vertigo.

(e) Emergency procedures.

Performance Standard. CCUI will demonstrate the ability to successfully crew the aircraft to the deck for a minimum of 5 landings while wearing NVGs under low level conditions.

Prerequisite. NVG-301.

NVG-303   1.5   R   1 HH-46D/E   NS

Goal. Develop proficiency in low level navigation and confined area landings. This flight may be conducted in HLL or LLL.

Requirement. CCUI will act in the capacity of the crew chief. CCUI will demonstrate proficiency while utilizing NVGs during navigation and CALs. CCUI will assist pilots with navigation by map and terrain features. Demonstrate operation and limitations of Night Sun search light during search patterns.

Brief/Discuss

(a) Lookout Doctrine.

(b) NVG scan techniques.

(c) Night Sun search light and it's effects on NVGs.

(d) Vertigo.

(e) Emergency procedures.

Performance Standard. CCUI shall demonstrate ability to assist pilots in navigation routes and search pattern, maintain good search doctrine, assist pilots to remain oriented on route within 500 meters, ensure effective CRM for navigation and obstacle clearance, and utilize proper terminology.

Prerequisite. NVG-302.

2. Night Search and Rescue

    a. Purpose. Develop the trainee's proficiency in loading, in-flight procedures, SAR procedures and requirements, SAR equipment utilization and limitations, and knowledge of safety regulations in the night environment.
    b. Safety. Rappels and short-hauls shall not be conducted while using NVGs.

    c. Crew Requirement. CCNSSI/CCUI.

    d. Prerequisite. Crew Chiefs may begin the night SAR syllabus training prior to completion of the entire day SAR syllabus. Prior to commencement of a night SAR syllabus flight, the corresponding day SAR syllabus flight shall be completed.

    e. Flight Training (8 flights, 12.5 Hours)

NSAR-320   1.5   R   1 HH-46D/E   N

Goal. Conduct night overland search.

Requirement. The CCUI, acting in the capacity of the crew chief, will demonstrate the crew chiefs duties during night, overland search operations and approach training utilizing standard ICS voice communications, the Night Sun search light, and the Remote Hover Coupler Station.   The CCUI will complete a minimum of 2 night manual approaches.

Performance Standard.   CCUI shall assist the pilots in conducting a search pattern consisting of a minimum of 5 checkpoints, maintaining within 500 meters of course line.   CCUI shall provide calls to the pilot to conduct a hover for crewmember deployment, maintaining within 5 feet of hover point.

Prerequisite.   SAR-252.

NSAR-321   1.5   R   1 HH-46D/E   N

Goal.   Conduct night over land hoisting operations utilizing the Rescue Strop, Forest Penetrator, Rescue Litter, MEDEVAC Litter, Rescue Net, and Hoisting Vest (if available).

Requirement.   The CCNSSI will introduce night, overland SAR procedures per NWP-3-50, utilization of SAR equipment, and utilization of chemical lights and chemical light straps.   The CCUI, acting in the capacity of the crew chief, will demonstrate the deployment and recovery of the Rescue Strop, Forest Penetrator, Rescue Litter, MEDEVAC Litter, Rescue Net, and Hoisting Vest in a confined area.   Review standard ICS voice communications and safety procedures.   Review hand, arm, and Aldis Lamp signals.

Performance Standard.   CCUI shall provide calls to the pilot to conduct a hover for crewmember deployment, maintaining within 5 feet of hover point.   The CCUI will safely conduct hoisting operations utilizing the Rescue Strop, Forest Penetrator, Rescue Litter, MEDEVAC Litter, Rescue Net, and Hoisting Vest.

Prerequisite.   SAR-253.

NSAR-322   2.0   R   1 HH-46D/E   N

Goal.   Conduct night, overland SAR exercise.   Assist the pilots with navigation and search.   Prepare the aircraft for accepting patients and/or survivors.   Assist the SARRACs with transporting patient/survivor to helicopter.

Requirement.   The CCUI, acting in the capacity of the crew chief, will demonstrate inland SAR procedures per NWP-3-50.   Demonstrate the deployment and recovery of rescue devices.   Demonstrate standard ICS voice communications.   Demonstrate hand, arm, and Aldis Lamp signals.   Demonstrate proper use and placement of the chemical lights and chemical light straps.

Performance Standard.   CCUI shall assist the pilots in navigation, provide calls to the pilot to conduct a hover for crewmember deployment, maintaining within 5 feet of hover point.   The CCUI will safely conduct hoisting operations, assist the SARRACs with patient transport to helicopter and secure patient into litter stanchions as required.

Prerequisite. SAR-255, NSAR-320, NSAR-321.

NSAR-323   1.5   R   1 HH-46D/E   N

Goal. Conduct night, over water SAR approach training.

Requirement. The CCNSSI will introduce night Doppler approaches, flare deployment, and discuss vertigo. The CCUI, acting in the capacity of the crew chief, will demonstrate the duties of the crew chief during night, manual and coupled Doppler approaches. Demonstrate use of the Remote Hover Coupler Station. Review standard ICS voice communications and safety procedures. The CCUI will complete a minimum of 2 night manual, and 2 night coupled approaches.

Performance Standard. CCUI shall provide calls to the pilot to conduct a hover for crewmember deployment, maintaining within 5 feet of hover point. The CCUI will safely conduct hoisting operations utilizing the Rescue Strop, Rescue Litter, MEDEVAC Litter, Rescue Net. CCUI will maintain a hover utilizing the Remote Hover Coupler Station, and maintain within 5 feet of hover point.

Prerequisite. SAR-256.

Ordnance. 1 Mk-25 Flare, 1Mk-58 Flare.

NSAR-330   1.5   R   1 HH-46D/E   N

Goal. Conduct night rescue swimmer deployments and recoveries utilizing the rescue strop, and rescue net.

Requirement. Review deployment and recovery procedures of rescue swimmer per NWP-3-50 and local SOP. The CCUI, acting in the capacity of the crew chief, will deploy and recover the rescue swimmer and simulated survivor(s) utilizing the rescue strop, and rescue net. Demonstrate proper flare deployment to mark swimmer/survivor position. Perform a short-haul operation. Review standard ICS voice communications and safety procedures. Review hand, arm, and Aldis Lamp signals. Review operation of the Remote Hover Coupler Station.

Performance Standard. CCUI shall provide calls to the pilot to conduct a hover for crewmember deployment, maintaining within 5 feet of hover point. The CCUI will safely conduct hoisting operations utilizing the rescue strop, and rescue net. CCUI will conduct 2 hovers utilizing the Remote Hover Coupler Station, and maintain hover within 5 feet of intended hover point.

Prerequisite. SAR-258, NSAR-320, NSAR-321, NSAR-323.

Ordnance. 1 Mk-25 Flare, 1 Mk-58 Flare.

NSAR-331   1.5   R   1 HH-46D/E   N

Goal. Conduct night rescue swimmer deployments and recoveries utilizing the stokes and SAR litter.

Requirement. Review deployment and recovery procedures of rescue swimmer per NWP-3-50 and local SOP. The CCUI, acting in the capacity of the crew chief, will deploy and recover the rescue swimmer and simulated survivor(s) utilizing the stokes and SAR litter. Demonstrate proper utilization of the Trail Line assembly. Demonstrate proper deployment of flares to mark swimmer/survivor position. Review standard ICS voice communications and safety procedures. Review hand, arm, and Aldis Lamp signals. Review operation of the Remote Hover Coupler Station.

Performance Standard. CCUI shall provide calls to the pilot to conduct a hover for crewmember deployment, maintaining within 5 feet of hover point. The CCUI will safely conduct hoisting operations utilizing the Rescue litter and MEDEVAC litter. CCUI will conduct 2 hovers utilizing the Remote Hover Coupler Station, and maintain hover within 5 feet of intended hover point.

Prerequisite. SAR-258, NSAR-320, NSAR-321, NSAR-323.

Ordnance. 1 Mk-25 Flare, 1 Mk-58 Flare.

NSAR-332   1.5   R   1 HH-46D/E   N

Goal. Conduct night SAR boat hoist training.

Requirement. The CCUI will act in the capacity of the crew chief. Conduct hoisting operations from a boat or ship with emphasis on the Rescue Litter, MEDEVAC Litter, and Trail Line assembly. Discuss normal and emergency procedures related to shipboard hoisting operations. Emphasize crew coordination and situational awareness as part of CRM brief. Review standard ICS voice communication and safety procedures. Review hand, arm, and Aldis Lamp signals. Review operation of the Remote Hover Coupler Station.

Performance Standard. CCUI shall provide calls to the pilot to conduct a hover over a boat for crewmember deployment, maintaining within 5 feet of hover point. The CCUI will safely conduct hoisting operations utilizing the stokes and SAR litters.

Prerequisite. SAR-260, NSAR-330 and 332.

NSAR-333   1.5   R   1 HH-46D/E   N

Goal. Practice night SAR boat hoist training.

Requirement. The CCUI will act in the capacity of the crew chief. Conduct hoisting operations from a boat or ship with emphasis on the stokes and SAR litters, and trail line assembly. Discuss normal and emergency procedures related to shipboard hoisting operations. Emphasize crew coordination and situational awareness as part of CRM brief. Review standard ICS voice communication and safety procedures. Review hand, arm, and Aldis Lamp signals. Review operation of the Remote Hover Coupler Station.

Performance Standard. CCUI shall provide calls to the pilot to conduct a hover over a boat for crewmember deployment, maintaining within 5 feet of hover point. The CCUI will safely conduct hoisting operations utilizing the stokes and SAR litters.

Prerequisite. SAR-260, NSAR-330.

SAR-340   2.0   R   1 HH-46D/E   N

Goal. Participate in night over water SAREX.

Requirement. The CCUI, acting in the capacity of the crew chief, will demonstrate proper utilization of rescue devices. Demonstrate proper deployment and recovery of rescue personnel and/or survivors. Demonstrate proper flare deployment. Demonstrate proper ICS voice communication and safety procedures. Demonstrate hand, arm, and Aldis Lamp signals. Demonstrate operation of the Remote Hover Coupler Station.

Performance Standard. CCUI shall assist the pilots in navigation, provide calls to the pilot to conduct a hover for crewmember deployment, maintaining within 5 feet of hover point. The CCUI will safely conduct hoisting operations, assist the RS and IFMT with patient transport to helicopter and secure patient into litter stanchions as required.

Prerequisite. SAR-255, NSAR-320 through NSAR-333.

Ordnance. 1 Mk-25 Flare, 1 Mk-58 Flare.

233. CORE PLUS TRAINING

1. Helicopter Inland Rescue Aircrewman (HIRA) Rappel Operations

a. Purpose. Develop the Crew Chief knowledge and proficiency of rappel procedures, equipment limitations, equipment set-up and usage, and safety checks.

b. General

(1) The Crew Chief may act in the capacity of a Crew Chief during rappel and short haul operations once he/she has completed RAP-400 and 402.

(2) To instruct RAP events a Crew Chief must have completed Helicopter Rappel Training Ground School (HSC-3) as required by OPNAVINST 3130.6 (series) and RAP-400, 401, 402, and 403 to be designated a HIRA Instructor.

(3) Prior to commencing HIRA Instructor flight training, the Crew Chief shall complete a local rappel ground-training syllabus and meet all requirements as indicated in applicable SAR related publications.

(4) All rappel-training evolutions shall be conducted with the use of the belay line for "Bagless" rappels or a HIRA qualified safety observer tending the free end of the rappel rope during a "Standard" rappel.

(5) Only HIRA qualified personnel shall act as a survivor for all training short haul evolutions.

(6) Rappel and hoisting operations should not be conducted while using NVGs.

(7) Upon completion of this stage of training, the Crew Chief should be able to correctly perform all required equipment set-ups and safely rappel from the helicopter.

c. Crew Requirements. HIRAI/HIRAUT.

d. Flight Training (4 flights, 6 hours)

RAP-400   1.5   1 HH-46D/E

Goal. Introduce SAR rappelling operations.

Requirement

(1) Brief/Discuss

(a) Safety considerations.

(b) Crew coordination and communication during rappel operations to include standard ICS terminology and hand and arm signals.

(c) Equipment inventory, preflight inspection and set-up.

(2) Introduce/Demonstrate

(a) Rappel rope and belay line rigging and setups.

(b) Conduct a minimum of 3 rappel descents, 2 standard rappels and 1 bagless rappel.

(c) Demonstrate the 3 "Lock-off" techniques.

Performance Standard. The CCUI should properly setup the rappel and belay line and conduct safety checks and observe/conduct 3 rappel descents.

RAP-401   1.5   1 HH-46D/E

Goal. Conduct SAR rappelling operations and introduce short haul procedures.

Requirement

(1) Brief/Discuss

(a) Safety considerations.

(b) Crew coordination and communication during rappel operations to include standard ICS terminology and hand and arm signals.

(c) Equipment inventory, preflight inspection and set-up.

(d) Short haul procedures and lock-off techniques.

(e) Hoisting Vest.

(2) Introduce/Demonstrate

(a) Rappel rope and belay line rigging and setups.

(b) Short haul procedures and use of hoisting vest.

(c) Conduct a minimum of 3 rappel descents with 1 ending and a short haul of a survivor in the hoisting vest.

Performance Standard. The CCUI should properly setup the rappel and belay line and conduct safety checks. The CCUI should perform 3 rappel descents and 1 short haul operation.

Prerequisite. RAP-400.

RAP-402   1.5   R   1 HH-46D/E

Goal. Conduct/observe SAR rappelling and short haul operations.

Requirement

(1) Brief/Discuss

(a) Safety considerations.

(b) Crew coordination and communication during rappel operations to include standard ICS terminology and hand and arm signals.

(c) Equipment inventory, preflight inspection and set-up.

(d) Short haul procedures and lock-off techniques.

(e) Rappelling with equipment and short haul procedures with the rescue litter.

(2) Introduce/Demonstrate

(a) Rappel rope and belay line rigging and setups.

(b) Conduct/observe a minimum of 3 rappel descents with equipment.

(c) Two descents should end with the short haul of a simulated survivor in the rescue litter.

Performance Standard. The CCUI should properly setup the rappel and belay line and conduct safety checks. The CCUI should perform/observe 3 rappel descents and 1 short haul operation of a simulated survivor in the Stokes litter.

Prerequisite. RAP-401.

RAP-403   1.5   R   1 HH-46D/E

Goal. Conduct HIRA Evaluation.

Requirement

(1) Brief/Discuss

(a) Safety considerations.

(b) Crew coordination and communication during rappel operations to include standard ICS terminology and hand and arm signals.

(c) Equipment inventory, preflight inspection and set-up.

(d) Short haul procedures and lock-off techniques.

(2) Introduce/Demonstrate

(a) Rappel rope and belay line rigging and setups.

(b) Standard and bag-less rappels with equipment.

(c) Conduct a minimum of 2 rappel descents with each ending with a short haul of a simulated survivor in the rescue litter.

Performance Standard. The CCUI should properly setup the rappel and belay line and conduct safety checks without assistance. The CCUI should perform 2 rappel descents ending in short haul operations of a simulated survivor in the Stokes litter.

Prerequisite. RAP-402.

2. Carrier Qualification

a. Purpose. Qualify during day and night shipboard landings.

b. General. Training includes FCLP/CQ and NVG operations. Extended searches may require shipboard operations for refueling, casualty recovery, and/ or remote site launches. The benefits of NVG operations cannot be over emphasized, and every effort should be made to ensure all crew members are SAR Night Systems Qualified (NSQ).

(1) Refer to the NATOPS Manual, NWP 3-04.1 (Helicopter Operations for Air Capable Ships), and LHA/LPH/LHD NATOPS.

(2) Pilots who are CQ current in the model H-46 helicopter will be considered current in the HH-46D/E until that currency expires.

(3) Five day and five NVD landings required for qualification/currency.

c. Crew Requirement

(1) Day flights. CCI/CCUI.

(2) Night flights. CCNSSI/CCUI.

d. <u>Flight Training (4 flights, 6 hours)</u>

FCLP-410   <u>1.5</u>   <u>R</u>   1 HH-46D/E

<u>Goal</u>. Conduct day, carrier pattern familiarization.

<u>Requirement</u>. Introduce day, FCLP patterns, approaches, and emergency procedures peculiar to shipboard operations. Discuss aircrew coordination, verbal/visual communications used during shipboard landings and launches, LSE signals, water landing/ditching, and aircraft lighting.

<u>Performance Standard</u>. The CCUI, acting in the capacity of the crew chief, shall demonstrate the ability/knowledge to perform shipboard flight operations to include LSE hand and arm signals.

FCLP-411   <u>1.5</u>   <u>R</u>   1 HH-46D/E   NS

<u>Goal</u>. Conduct NVG carrier pattern familiarization.

<u>Requirement</u>. Introduce NVG FCLP patterns, approaches, landings, and emergency procedures peculiar to shipboard operations. Discuss aircrew coordination, crew comfort levels, situational awareness, verbal/visual communications used during shipboard landings and launches, LSE signals, water landing/ditching, and aircraft lighting.

<u>Performance Standard</u>. The CCUI, acting in the capacity of the crew chief, shall demonstrate the ability/knowledge to perform night shipboard flight operations to include night LSE hand and arm signals.

<u>Prerequisite</u>. FLCP-410.

CQ-420   <u>1.5</u>   <u>R</u>   1 HH-46D/E

<u>Goal</u>. Conduct day, carrier qualifications.

<u>Requirement</u>. Introduce CQ patterns, approaches, landings, and emergency procedures particular to shipboard operations. Discuss height over various decks, aircrew coordination, verbal/visual communications used during shipboard landings and launches, LSE signals, water landing/ditching, and aircraft lighting. Introduce day carrier qualification per NATOPS.

<u>Performance Standard</u>. The CCUI, acting in the capacity of the crew chief, shall demonstrate the ability/knowledge to perform shipboard flight operations to include LSE hand and arm signals.

<u>Prerequisite</u>. FCLP-410.

CQ-421   1.5   R   1 HH-46D/E   NS

   Goal. Conduct NVG carrier qualifications.

   Requirement. Introduce NVG CQ patterns, approaches, landings, and emergency procedures particular to shipboard operations. Discuss height over various decks, deck lighting, aircrew coordination, verbal/visual communications used during shipboard landings and launches, LSE signals, water landing/ditching, and aircraft lighting.

   Performance Standard. The CCUI, acting in the capacity of the crew chief, shall demonstrate the ability/knowledge to perform night shipboard flight operations to include night LSE hand and arm signals.

   Prerequisite. FCLP-411.

240. CREW CHIEF INSTRUCTOR UNDER TRAINING (CCIUT) SAR NATOPS/ASSISTANT NATOPS INSTRUCTOR

1. Crew Chief Instructor Under Training

  a. Purpose. Develop qualified instructor Crew Chiefs with the ability to teach SAR operations and standardize the procedures for qualifying instructors within individual units.

  b. General

   (1) The CCIUT must demonstrate proficiency in instructing all evolutions in this stage.

   (2) Upon completion of this stage the CCIUT shall be designated a Crew Chief Instructor (CCI).

  c. Crew Requirements. CCI/CCIUT.

  d. Prerequisites. All Core Skill Introduction, Basic, and Advanced Training must be complete.

  e. Flight Training (3 flights, 6 hours)

IUT-500   1.5   E   1 HH-46D/E

   Goal. Demonstrate instructional techniques during day FAM/EP/CAL/INT sorties.

   Requirement. CCIUT will demonstrate instructional techniques in crew responsibilities during preflight, start, taxi, take-off, landing, in-flight emergency procedures, ICS procedures, and confined area landings.

IUT-503   1.5   E   1 HH-46D/E

   Goal. Demonstrate instructional techniques during water bucket operations.

Requirement. The CCIUT will demonstrate instructional techniques during water bucket operations emphasizing cargo hook operation and limitations, load stability, emergency procedures, lookout doctrine, crew coordination, ICS procedures, and obstacle clearance.

IUT-504   3.0   E   1 HH-46D/E   (N)

Goal. Demonstrate instructional techniques during SAR operations. This flight may be flown in day or night environment.

Requirement. The CCIUT will demonstrate instructional techniques in crew responsibilities and procedures during SAR operations, emphasizing SAR procedures, hoist operations, crew coordination, safety, ICS procedures, obstacle clearance, and flare deployment.

Prerequisites. IUT-500, IUT-503.

Ordnance. 4 Mk-58 Flare as required.

241. INSTRUCTOR UNDER TRAINING (GRADUATE LEVEL: NSSI)

1. Crew Chief Night System SAR Instructor (NSSI)

    a. The Crew Chief Night System SAR Instructor (NSSI) Course and training codes are listed in the MAWTS-1 Course Catalog. There will be no refly factors for these instructor flights.

    b. A NSSI is a Crew Chief who has completed the NVG syllabus, certified by a NSI and designated by his squadron commanding officer. Designated NSSI's are qualified to instruct all NVG flights.

    c. Previous qualifications represent a wealth of experience in NVG operations which may enhance the capabilities of a SAR unit. Crew Chiefs that have completed the SAR and NVG syllabi and meet the following criteria shall be eligible for the NSSI syllabus:

        (1) SAR Crew Chief Instructor (CCI) designation.

        (2) Fifty hours minimum of NVG time.

        (3) Twenty-five hours minimum of NVG time under LLL conditions.

    d. Crew Chiefs previously designated as NSI who are current in the CH-46E may be designated a NSSI following completion of the SAR and IUT syllabi.

    e. Standardization shall be accomplished during MAWTS-1 certification flights and annual SAR evaluations.

NSSI-551: See MAWTS Course Catalog.

NSSI-552: See MAWTS Course Catalog.

NSSI-553: See MAWTS Course Catalog.

250. REQUIREMENTS, QUALIFICATIONS AND DESIGNATIONS

1. Requirements, Qualifications, and Designations

    a. Purpose. Ensure standardization of HH-46D/E crew chief in normal operations, emergency and SAR procedures.

    b. General. RQD-600 is an annual OPNAVINST 3710.7 requirement. Once an air crewman becomes SAR designated, RQD-602 may be flown in conjunction with RQD-600. RQD-640 is the CRM flight and may be flown in conjunction with the RQD-600 and/or RQD-602. RQD-604 is a Functional Check Flight code that is designed to indicate a crew chief has completed a locally generated FCF syllabus and is proficient in Functional Check Flight operations.

    c. Crew Requirements

        (1) CCI/CCUI if flights are flown during day.

        (2) CCNSSI/CCUI if flights are flown at night.

    d. Flight Training (3 flights, 6 hours)

RQD-600   1.5   E   1 HH-46D/E   (N)

    Goal. NATOPS evaluation.

    Requirements. Perform an evaluated flight per the HH-46D/E NATOPS Flight Manual. A NATOPS/Assistant NATOPS Instructor is required for this flight.

    Performance Standard. The performance expected by the evaluator in this flight shall be commensurate with the experience of the aircrew under evaluation.

    Prerequisite. The NATOPS open book and closed book exams shall be completed prior to this flight.

RQD-602   3.0   E   1 HH-46D/E   (N)

    Goal. SAR evaluation.

    Requirements. The crew chief will demonstrate the ability to perform all tasks outlined in the NATOPS Flight Manual, with particular emphasis on the SAR mission. The check ride shall cover all aspects of the local SAR mission, NWP-3-50, and local SOP. A NATOPS/Assistant NATOPS Instructor is required for this flight.

    Performance Standard. The performance expected by the evaluator in this flight shall be commensurate with the experience of the aircrew under evaluation.

    Prerequisite. Prior to this flight the CCUI shall complete the Mission Capable, Mission Ready, and Mission Qualification stages of training. The NATOPS open book and closed book tests shall also be completed prior to this flight. RQD-600.

Ordnance. 1 Mk-25 Flare, 1 Mk-58 Flare.

RQD-604   1.5   E   1 HH-46D/E

Goal. Develop proficiency in Functional Check Flight (FCF) procedures and operations.

General. This flight does not require a CCI. However, the trainee shall perform the flight under the supervision and guidance of a FCF qualified crew chief.

Requirement. The CCUI will demonstrate knowledge and proficiency of FCF procedures, equipment installation and operation, adjustments to necessary components, and aircraft systems operating limitations.

Performance Standard. The CCIU will satisfactorily perform two FCF Full cards.

Prerequisites. The CCUI shall complete a locally generated FCF syllabus.

RQD-640   1.5   E   1 HH-46D/E   (N)

Goal. Conduct a Crew Resource Management (CRM) evaluation.

Crew Requirement. CRMI or CRMF/CCUI.

Requirement. Crew chief will be evaluated on demonstration of knowledge and application of the principles of CRM.

Performance Standard. CCUI shall safely demonstrate CRM principles while executing a simulated mission scenario.

260. TRAINING RESOURCES (EXPENDABLE ORDNANCE). The below ordnance requirements are based on a "per crew" basis per OPNAVNOTE 8010.

ORDNANCE	200 SERIES	300 SERIES	500 SERIES	600 SERIES	ANNUAL*
Mk-25 Flares	2	4	1	1	8
Mk-58 Flares	2	4	1	1	8

* Annual ordnance requirements maintain an aircrew member at 85% MRP per T&R Program Manual.

261. SYLLABUS MATRICES. These matrices display specific event information such as; flight/simulator hours, refly interval, prerequisites, CRP, chaining, etc.

									HH-46D/E SAR CREW CHIEF				
									CORE SKILL BASIC (200 SERIES)				
STAGE	TRNG CODE	FLT HOURS	SIM HOURS	REFLY INTERVAL	POI	EVAL	TOTAL A/C	TYPE	CONDITIONS	PREQ	EVENT DESC	CRP	CHAINING	EVENT CONV
						OFT								
FAM	203	1.5		*	R		1	A			AREA FAM	1.00		108
FAM	204	1.5		*	SC,R		1	A			"E" – EP FAM	1.00		109
FAM	205	1.5		*	R		1	A			"D" – EP FAM	1.00		
		4.5	0.0									3.00		
						FAM/EP								
CAL	220	1.5		*	R		1	A			DAY CAL	1.00		120
		1.5	0.0									1.00		
						INT								
INT	230	1.5		*	SC,R		1	A			"E" – INT CARGO	1.00		130
INT	231	1.5		*	R		1	A			REV INT CARGO	1.00		
		3.0	0.0									2.00		
						FF								
FF	240	1.5		*	R		1	A			BAMBI BUCKET	0.50		140
		1.5	0.0									0.50		
						SAR								
SAR	250	1.5		365	R		1	A		203,204, 205,220, 231	GPS NAV	0.50		200
SAR	252	1.5		365	R		1	A		203,204, 205,220, 231	DAY SEARCH	1.00		202
SAR	253	1.5		365	R		1	A		203,204, 205,220, 231	DAY LAND HOIST	1.00		203
SAR	254	1.5		365	R		1	A		253	DAY RAMP HOIST	1.00		204
SAR	255	1.5		365	R		1	A		250,252, 253	DAY SAREX	1.00	253,252, 251,250, 220	205
SAR	256	1.5		365	R		1	A			DAY DOPPLER	1.00		206
SAR	258	1.5		365	R		1	A		253,256	DAY WATER WORK (STROP)	1.00	256	207
SAR	259	1.5		365	R		1	A		258	DAY WATER WORK (LITTER)	1.00	256	208
SAR	260	1.5		365	R		1	A		253,256, 258	DAY BOAT HOIST	1.00	259,258, 256	209
		13.5	0.0									8.50		
						PHASE TOTAL								
FLT HRS		24.0	0.0	SIM HRS								15.00	CRP TOTAL	

	HH-46D/E SAR CREW CHIEF
	CORE SKILL ADVANCED (300 SERIES)
STAGE	TRNG CODE	FLT HOURS	SIM HOURS	REFLY INTERVAL	POI	EVAL	TOTAL A/C	TYPE	CONDITION	PREQ	EVENT DESC	CRP	CHAINING	EVENT CONV
	NVG
NVG	300	1.5		365	R		1	A	NS	200,201,202, 220	NVG HLL FAM	1.50		300
NVG	301	1.5		365	R		1	A	NS	300	NVG CAL	1.50	300	301
NVG	302	1.5		365	R		1	A	NS	301	NVG NAV	1.50	301,300	302
NVG	303	1.5		365	R		1	A	NS	302	NVG NAV & CAL	2.00	300,301,302	303
		6.0	0.0									6.50		
	NSAR
NSAR	320	1.5		365	R		1	A	N	252	NIGHT LAND SEARCH	1.50	302,301,300, 252	321
NSAR	321	1.5		365	R		1	A	N	253	NIGHT LAND HOIST	1.00	302,301,300, 253	322
NSAR	322	2.0		365	R		1	A	N	255,320,321	NIGHT LAND SAREX	2.00	321,320,302, 301,300,255, 253,252,251, 250,220	323
NSAR	323	1.5		365	R		1	A	N	256	NIGHT DOPPLER	1.00	302,300,256	324
NSAR	330	1.5		365	R		1	A	N	258,320,321, 323	NIGHT WATER WORKS (STROP)	1.00	323,302,300, 258,256	235
NSAR	331	1.5		365	R		1	A	N	258,320,321, 323	NIGHT WATER WORKS (LITTER)	1.00	323,302,300, 259,256	326
NSAR	332	1.5		365	R		1	A	N	260,330	NIGHT BOAT HOIST	2.00	331,302,300, 260,259	327
NSAR	333	1.5		365	R		1	A	N	260,330,332	REV NIGHT BOAT HOIST	2.00	332,331,302, 300,260,259	
NSAR	340	2.0		365	R		1	A	N	255,331,333	NIGHT WATER SAREX	2.00	331,330,323, 302,300,256	328
		14.5	0.0									13.50		
	PHASE TOTAL
FLT HRS		20.5	0.0	SIM HRS	colspan=7		20.00	CRP TOTAL	

STAGE	TRNG CODE	FLT HOURS	SIM HOURS	REFLY INTERVAL	POI	EVAL	TOTAL A/C	TYPE	CONDITIONS	PREQ	EVENT DESC	CRP	CHAINING	EVENT CONV
							HH-46D/E SAR CREW CHIEF							
							CORE PLUS (400 SERIES)							
							RAP							
RAP	400	1.5		365	R		1	A			INTRO RAPPEL	0.50		400
RAP	401	1.5		365	R		1	A		400	RAPPEL & SHORT HAUL	0.50	400	502
RAP	402	1.5		30	R		1	A		401	RAPPEL & SHORT HAUL	0.50	400	
RAP	403	1.5		365	R		1	A		402	HIRA EVAL	0.50		
		6.0	0.0									2.00		
							FCLP							
FCLP	410	1.5		365	R		1	A			DAY FCLP	0.50		410
FCLP	411	1.5		365	R		1	A	NS	410	NIGHT FCLP	0.50	410	411
		3.0	0.0									1.00		
							CQ							
CQ	420	1.5		365	R		1	A		410	DAY CQ	1.00	410	420
CQ	421	1.5		365	R		1	A	NS		NIGHT CQ	1.00	420,411,410	421
		3.0	0.0									2.00		
							PHASE TOTAL							
FLT HRS		12.0	0.0	SIM HRS								5.00	CRP TOTAL	

STAGE	TRNG CODE	FLT HOURS	SIM HOURS	REFLY INTERVAL	POI	EVAL	TOTAL A/C	TYPE	CONDITIONS	PREQ	EVENT DESC	CRP	CHAINING	EVENT CONV
							INSTRUCTOR TRAINING (500 SERIES)							
							IUT							
IUT	500	1.5		*		X	1	A			IUT FAM	0.00		500
IUT	503	1.5		*		X	1	A			IUT WATER BUCKET	0.00		502
IUT	504	1.5		*		X	1	A		500,503	IUT EVAL	0.00		503
		4.5	0.0									0.00		
							NSSI							
NSSI	551	1.5		*		X	1	A	NS		NSSI HLL	0.00		
NSSI	552	1.5		*		X	1	A	NS		NSSI LLL	0.00		
NSSI	553	1.5		*		X	1	A	NS	551,552	NSSI EVAL	0.00		
		4.5	0.0									0.00		
							PHASE TOTAL							
FLT HRS		9.0	0.0	SIM HRS								0.00	CRP TOTAL	

										HH-46D/E SAR CREW CHIEF			
										REQUIREMENTS, QUALIFICATIONS, & DESIGNATIONS [RQD] (600 SERIES)			
STAGE	TRNG CODE	FLT HOURS	SIM HOURS	REFLY INTERVAL	POI	EVAL	TOTAL A/C	TYPE	CONDITION	PREQ	EVENT DESC	CRP	CHAINING	EVENT CONV
											RQD			
RQD	600	3.0		365		X	1	A	(N)		NATOPS EVAL	0.00		600
RQD	602	3.0		365		X	1	A	(N)	600	SAR EVAL	0.00	600	602
RQD	604	1.5		*		X	1	A			FCF	0.00		603
RQD	640	1.5		365		X	1	A	(N)		CRM EVAL	0.00		640
		9.0	0									0.00		
								PHASE TOTAL						
FLT HRS		9.0	0	SIM HRS								0.00	CRP TOTAL	

SYLLABUS EVENT CONVERSION MATRIX

OLD STAGE	OLD TRNG CODE	NEW STAGE	NEW TRNG CODE
		200 LEVEL	
FAM	108	FAM	200
EP	109	EP "E"	201
		EP "D"	202
CAL	120	CAL	220
INT	130	INT "E"	230
		INT "D"	231
FF	140	FF	240

OLD STAGE	OLD TRNG CODE	NEW STAGE	NEW TRNG CODE
		200 LEVEL	
SAR	200	SAR	250
	202		252
	203		253
	204		254
	205		255
	206		256
	207		258
	208		259
	209		260

Figure 2-1.--Crew Chief Syllabus Conversion Matrix.

SYLLABUS EVENT CONVERSION MATRIX

OLD STAGE	OLD TRNG CODE	NEW STAGE	NEW TRNG CODE
	300 LEVEL		
NVG	300	NVG	300
	301		301
	302		302
	303		303
NSAR	321	NSAR	320
	322		321
	323		322
	324		323
	235		330
	326		331
	327		332
			333
	328		340

OLD STAGE	OLD TRNG CODE	NEW STAGE	NEW TRNG CODE
	400 LEVEL		
RAP	400	RAP	400
	502		402
FCLP	410	FCLP	410
	411		411
CQ	420	CQ	420
	421		421

Figure 2-1.--Crew Chief Syllabus Conversion Matrix--Continued.

SYLLABUS EVENT CONVERSION MATRIX

OLD STAGE	OLD TRNG CODE	NEW STAGE	NEW TRNG CODE
	500 LEVEL		
IUT	500	IUT	500
	502		503
	503		504

OLD STAGE	OLD TRNG CODE	NEW STAGE	NEW TRNG CODE
	600 LEVEL		
RQD	600	RQD	600
	602		602
	603		604
	640		640

Figure 2-1.--Crew Chief Syllabus Conversion Matrix--Continued.

CHAPTER 3

HH-46D/E SAR RESCUE AIRCREWMAN (SARRAC)

* * N O T E * *

*Aircrews shall include Aircrew Coordination Techniques and/or
Crew Resource Management as part of their brief.*

CHAPTER 3

HH-46D SAR RESCUE AIRCREWMAN (SARRAC)

300. MARINE SEARCH AND RESCUE UNIT - HH-46D/E

1. General. The capabilities defined and described in the core capability and unit template sections are provided to ensure each SAR unit maintains a common base of training and depth of capabilities. When sources permit, and when, in the judgment of the commander, additional training would significantly increase the unit's Search and Rescue capability, training to a level above these base capabilities is permitted. It is incumbent upon and expected of commanders to balance any increase in the depth of core capabilities against the long-term health and readiness of their unit while staying within resource constraints.

2. Mission. The primary mission of Search and Rescue is to provide heliborne SAR capabilities to tenant aviation units. Additional missions are secondary in nature and shall be accepted on a not-to-interfere basis only.

3. Mission Essential Task List (METL)

    a. Provide search and rescue for tenant aircraft.

    b. Provide supplemental search and rescue asset for U. S. Coast Guard and U.S. Air Force.

    c. Provide MEDEVAC capability to local civilian agencies as requested, on a not-to-interfere basis.

    d. Provide airborne fire-fighting capability for MCAS facilities and to supplement local area Forest Service assets.

    e. Provide supplemental search and rescue to local civilian agencies for non-law enforcement type missions such as searches, fire fighting, disaster response, or civilian MEDEVAC, when civilian agencies cannot respond.

    f. Provide utility and logistics support missions of MCAS activities as directed by the Director of Operations, Marine Corps Installations (MCI) EAST.

    g. Enhance public relations for the Commanding General, MCI EAST through static displays and flight demonstrations as authorized by higher authority.

4. Table of Organization

                        3 HH-46D/E helicopters
                        8 Pilots
                        9 Crew Chiefs
                        6 SAR Swimmers
                        4 SAR Corpsmen

5. Squadron Core Capability

    a. A core capable squadron is able to sustain the following minimum performance on a daily basis during sustained search and rescue operations, assuming at least 100% Primary Authorized Allowance (PAA), 90% in reporting status, and 90% T/O on hand in all MOSs. If <90%, core capability will be degraded by like-percentage. The extent to which a core capable squadron is able to surge beyond its core capability is situational dependent.

   b. A core capable squadron is able to launch 1 full mission capable aircraft crewed by a fully qualified aircrew at all times. This aircraft must be airborne within 15 minutes of alert when operating under SAR Condition I and 1 hour under SAR Condition II.

301. PROGRAMS OF INSTRUCTION (POI)

1. The Basic POI is for all SARRAC's assigned for their first time to a SAR unit utilizing the HH-46 aircraft.

2. The Refresher POI is for all SARRAC's who have previously been assigned to a SAR unit utilizing the HH-46 aircraft. Personnel who have previously been assigned duties as a SARRAC in another platform must complete the Basic POI.

3. The SARRAC aircrew position does not require a series conversion syllabus between the HH-46d and HH-46E.

302. POI FOR BASIC SARRAC

WEEKS	COURSE/PHASE	ACTIVIT
4	Naval Aircrew Candidate School	NAS Pensacola
6	Rescue Swimmer School	NAS Pensacola
2	Ground Training	VMR-1
17	Flight Training	VMR-1

303. POI FOR REFRESHER SARRAC

WEEKS	COURSE/PHASE	ACTIVITY
2	SAR Ground Training	VMR-1
10	SAR Flight Training	VMR-1

304. POI FOR INSTRUCTOR UNDER TRAINING

WEEKS	COURSE/PHASE	
3	SAR IUT Flight Training	VMR-1

   *SARRAC's do not have an NSSI qualification, initial NVD training is conducted by SAR Crew Chief NSSI's.

305. SQUADRON LEVEL TRAINING

   NATOPS Flight Manual and NATOPS Pocket Checklist
   Search and Rescue (SAR) Publications
   Safety Publications
   Squadron Standard Operating Procedures (SOPs)
   Inspection, Utilization, and Limitations of Personal Aviation Survival
   Equipment
   Inspection, Utilization, and Limitations of SAR Equipment
   Inspection, Utilization, and Limitations of SAR Medical Equipment
   Hand and Arm Signals
   Search and Rescue Techniques
   CPR Certification
   Helicopter Rappel Training Manual (Student Guide)

Fire Bucket (Bambi Bucket) Operations Manual
Night Vision Device Ground Training
Ordnance Safety

306. FLIGHT TRAINING POI FOR BASIC SARRAC

1. SAR Rescue Air Crewman (SARRAC) encompass both the SAR Medical Technician (MedTech) and the SAR Rescue Swimmer. Each Basic SARRAC will be programmed to fly the complete program of instruction.

2. All syllabus flights shall be flown with a designated SARRAC NATOPS/Assistant NATOPS Instructor.

307. FLIGHT TRAINING FOR REFRESHER SARRAC

1. Previously qualified SARRACs will be required to fly the appropriate Program of Instruction.

2. Consideration may be given to previous experience and qualifications. The POI shall be developed on an individual basis and include at a minimum the flights listed in the syllabus matrix. The commanding officer may waive flights per the T&R Program Manual, NAVMC DIR 3500.14_.

3. All flights shall be flown with a designated SARRAC NATOPS/Assistant NATOPS Instructor.

308. REQUIREMENTS FOR SARRAC DESIGNATION

1. Complete all eighteen academic lectures.

2. Complete SAR Open Book Examination, NATOPS Open and Closed Book Examination, and SAR Fitness Test.

3. T&R Codes complete through 340 for Rescue Swimmers, 341 for Medical Technicians.

4. NATOPS Evaluation, SARRAC/HIRA Evaluation and CRM Evaluation (T&R Codes 600, 602 and 640).

320. GROUND/ACADEMIC TRAINING

COURSE	ACTIVITY
Naval Aircrew Candidate School	NAS Pensacola
Rescue Swimmer School	NAS Pensacola
Helicopter Rappel Indoctrination Course*	HC-3 NAS N Island
Emergency Medical Technician Training	Naval Hospital

*Completion of the Rappel Indoctrination Course and Emergency Medical Technician Training is highly recommended but not required.

330. FLIGHT PERFORMANCE REQUIREMENTS

1. Purpose. Promote standardization of SARRAC procedures and to establish a minimum training program for those personnel assigned as a SARRAC aboard the HH-46D/E.

2. General

    a. Personnel shall complete the Naval Aircrew Candidate School and Rescue Swimmer School prior to commencement of flight training.

    b. Personnel should complete Helicopter Rappel Indoctrination Course as soon as possible. Personnel are required to complete Helicopter Rappel Indoctrination Course prior to commencement of Helicopter Inland Rescue Aircrewmen (HIRA) training.

    c. All flights shall terminate with a comprehensive debrief with emphasis on the aircrew's performance using all evaluation techniques.

    d. Aircrews should fly events annotated with an N at least 30 minutes after official sunset. Pilots may fly events annotated with (N) at night.

    e. Aircrews shall fly events annotated with an NS with Night Vision Devices (NVDs) for the entire flight. Aircrews may fly events with (NS) with the option of using NVDs.

    f. Environmental conditions (day or night) or Night Systems conditions shall be annotated in flight events and the syllabus matrix as follows:

Code	Requirement
D	Shall be flown or conducted during day.
N	Shall be flown or conducted at night (using available night vision devices or flown unaided).
(N)	May be flown or conducted day or night; if at night, available night vision devices may be used or flown unaided.
NS	Shall be flown or conducted at night using available night vision devices.
(NS)	May be flown or conducted day or night; if at night, available night vision devices shall be used.
N*	Event Shall be flown or conducted at night unaided.
(N*)	Event may be flown or conducted at night; if at night, shall be flown unaided.

3. Refly Interval. The syllabus matrix shows refly interval and Combat Readiness Percentage (CRP) for SARRACs.

4. Aircrew Evaluation Flights. All flights annotated with an E are required to have one of the following:

    a. NATOPS evaluation form filled out annually upon completion of the NATOPS Check (RQD-600).

    b. OPNAVINST 3130.6 evaluation form filled out annually upon completion of the SARRAC/HIRA Check (RDQ-601).

c. Any flight in the Core Skill Advanced, Core Skill Basic, or Core Plus phase as recommended by the Squadron Standardization Board.

5. <u>Aircrew Coordination/Crew Resource Management</u>. Aircrews shall include Crew Resource Management (CRM) as part of their mission brief. A CRM check flight will be conducted once annually

331. <u>CORE SKILL BASIC TRAINING</u>

1. <u>Familiarization</u>

    a. <u>Purpose</u>. Familiarize the SARRACUI with HH-46 operations and procedures.

    b. <u>General</u>. These flights may be flown on any appropriate flight of the pilot syllabus.

    c. <u>Crew Requirements</u>. SARRACI/SARRACUI.

    d. <u>Flight Training (2 Flights, 3.0 Hours)</u>

FAM-200   1.5   1 HH-46D/E

    <u>Goal</u>. Conduct an area and aircraft familiarization flight. Introduce HH-46 characteristics, SARRAC responsibilities, and discuss crew coordination.

    <u>Requirement</u>

    (1) <u>Brief/Discuss</u>

        (a) HH-46 nomenclature.

        (b) Preflight/Postflight procedures.

        (c) Equipment inventory and inspection.

        (d) Look-out doctrine.

    (2) <u>Introduce/Demonstrate</u>

        (a) Preflight/Postflight procedures.

        (b) Equipment inventory and inspection.

        (c) Look-out techniques and procedures.

    <u>Performance Standard</u>. SARRACUI shall become familiar with the local operating area and the HH-46.

EP-201   1.5   R   1 HH-46D/E

    <u>Goal</u>. Conduct emergency procedure familiarization and review area familiarization.

    <u>Requirement</u>

    (1) <u>Brief/Discuss</u>

        (a) HH-46D nomenclature.

(b) Preflight/Postflight procedures.

(c) Equipment inventory and inspection.

(d) Ground and In-flight emergencies.

(e) Ditching and Egress procedures.

(2) Introduce/Demonstrate

(a) Preflight/Postflight procedures to include Equipment inventory and inspection.

(b) Ground and In-flight emergencies.

(c) Ditching and Egress procedures.

Performance Standard. SARRACUI shall demonstrate knowledge of aircraft systems, perform basic FAM maneuvers, and be able to satisfactorily perform emergency procedures per NATOPS manual.

2. Confined Area Landings (CAL)

a. Purpose. Instruct the SARRACUI in his duties when landing in confined areas.

b. General. These flights may be flown on any flight of the pilot CAL stage.

c. Crew Requirements. SARRACI/SARRACUI.

d. Flight Training (1 Flights, 1.5 Hours)
CAL-220   1.5   1 HH-46D/E

Goal. Introduce day confined area landings.

Requirement

(1) Brief/Discuss

(a) HH-46D nomenclature to include specific blade clearance lengths and measurements.

(b) CAL zone evaluation.

(c) Crew Coordination and responsibilities to include obstacle avoidance lookout responsibilities.

(d) Standard voice communications and Lost ICS procedures

(e) Emergency procedures and departure routes.

(2) Introduce/Demonstrate

(a) HH-46 nomenclature to include specific blade clearance lengths and measurements.

(b) CAL zone selection and evaluation.

(c) Crew Coordination and responsibilities.

(d) Standard voice communications and lost ICS procedures.

(e) Emergency procedures and departure routes.

(f) Conduct at least 5 CALs with 3 being performed with the SARRACUI acting as the crew chief.

Performance Standard. SARRACUI will demonstrate the ability to successfully crew the aircraft to the deck for a minimum of 5 landings.

CAL-221   1.5   1 HH-46D/E

Goal. Practice day confined area landings.

Requirement

(1) Brief/Discuss

(a) HH-46D/E nomenclature to include specific blade clearance lengths and measurements.

(b) CAL zone evaluation.

(c) Crew Coordination and responsibilities to include obstacle avoidance lookout responsibilities.

(d) Standard voice communications and Lost ICS procedures

(e) Emergency procedures and departure routes.

(2) Introduce/Demonstrate

(a) HH-46 nomenclature to include specific blade clearance lengths and measurements.

(b) CAL zone selection and evaluation.

(c) Crew Coordination and responsibilities.

(d) Standard voice communications and lost ICS procedures.

(e) Emergency procedures and departure routes.

(f) Conduct at least 5 CALs with 3 being performed with the SARRACUI acting as the crew chief.

Performance Standard. SARRACUI will demonstrate the ability to successfully crew the aircraft to the deck for a minimum of 5 landings.

Prerequisite. CAL-220.

3. Internal Loads

    a. Purpose. Introduce the SARRACUI to patient, cargo and passenger loading and unloading procedures.

    b. General. These flights may be flown on any appropriate flight of the pilot syllabus.

c. Crew Requirements. SARRACI/SARRACUI.

d. Flight Training (2 Flights, 3.0 Hours)

INT-230   1.5   R   1 HH-46E

Goal. Review procedures for cargo loading and unloading.

Requirement

(1) Brief/Discuss

(a) Cargo loading/unloading procedures.

(b) Tie-down and securing cargo.

(2) Introduce/Demonstrate

(a) Cargo loading/unloading procedures.

(b) Tie-down and securing cargo.

Performance Standard. SARRACUI will demonstrate the ability to safely embark and debark passengers and cargo. SARRACUI will demonstrate the ability to safely refuel and manage in-flight responsibilities for the internal fuel tank.

INT-231   1.5   R   1 HH-46D

Goal. Review procedures for patient loading, passenger briefing and safety procedures.

Requirement

(1) Brief/Discuss

(a) Passenger manifesting and safety briefing.

(b) Patient loading.

(2) Introduce/Demonstrate

(a) Passenger manifesting and safety briefing.

(b) Patient loading.

Performance Standard. SARRACUI will demonstrate the ability to safely embark and debark litter patients.

Prerequisite. INT-230.

4. Fire Fighting

a. Purpose. Develop the ability to conduct water bucket operations.

b. General. These flights may be flown with water bucket flights in the pilot syllabus.

c. Crew Requirements. SARRACI/SARRACUI.

d. Flight Training (1 Flight, 1.5 Hours)

FF-240   1.5   R   1 HH-46D/E

Goal. Review procedures for water bucket (Bambi Bucket) operations.

Requirement

(1) Brief/Discuss

(a) Water bucket operations.

(b) Preflight/postflight procedures and limitations for external cargo hook and water bucket.

(c) Communication procedures to include standard terminology and hand and arm signals for lost ICS procedures.

(d) Emergency procedures to include lost ICS and Emergency cut-away (Pickle).

(2) Introduce/Demonstrate

(a) Preflight procedures and limitations for external cargo hook and water bucket.

(b) Equipment hook up and staging procedures.

(c) Communication procedures to include standard terminology and hand and arms signals for lost ICS procedures.

(d) Emergency procedures to include lost ICS and Emergency cut-away (Pickle).

(e) Postflight procedures and Bambi Bucket maintenance.

Performance Standard. SARRACUI shall be able to safely fill Bambi Bucket, complete minimum of 5 hookups and water drops, and deliver water to fire within 5 meters of intended point of impact.

5. Day Search and Rescue

a. Purpose. Familiarize the SARRACUI with the SAR mission and operations, aircraft limitations and emergency procedures. To develop proficiency in loading cargo/passengers, in-flight procedures, SAR procedures, requirements, and knowledge of safety regulations.

b. General. The T&R Program Manual addresses the commanding officer's authority to modify this training as required. Personnel will complete the appropriate ground schools prior to beginning the flight-training syllabus. A NATOPS instructor will monitor the SARRACUI's progress during the flight-training syllabus.

c. Crew Requirements. SARRACI/SARRACUI.

6. Navigation/Medical Evacuation (MEDEVAC)

    a. Purpose

        (1) Familiarize the SARRACUI with general navigational techniques while operating in the surrounding areas and area hospitals landing areas.

        (2) Familiarize and practice procedures for Medical Evacuation and providing continued care while enroute to a Medical Treatment Facility.

    b. General. The T&R Program Manual addresses the commanding officer's authority to modify this training as required. Personnel will complete the appropriate ground schools prior to beginning the flight training syllabus. A SARRAC NATOPS instructor will monitor the SARRACUIs progress during the flight-training syllabus.

    c. Prerequisite. The following flights of the HH-46D SARRAC syllabus shall be satisfactorily completed prior to commencing this stage: FAM-200, EP-201, CAL-221, INT-230 and 231.

    d. Crew Requirements. SARRACI/SARRACUI.

    e. Flight Training (6 Flights, 9.0 Hours)

SAR-250   1.5   1 HH-46D/E

        Goal. Introduce navigation procedures and local area hospital landing zones.

        Requirement

        (1) Brief/Discuss

            (a) Navigation procedures to include use of Global Positioning System (GPS) and aeronautical charts.

            (b) Area hospitals and their medical capabilities/locations.

            (c) Cabin preparation and rigging of the litters.

            (d) Use of radios in relaying patient information to the destination medical facility and use of the aircraft utility electrical power supply.

        (2) Introduce/Demonstrate

            (a) Identify local area hospital Landing Zones.

            (b) Use of aircraft electrical system and radio to contact receiving medical facility.

        Performance Standard. SARRACUI shall safely prepare the cabin for litter carriage using the stanchions, and should demonstrate the ability to utilize the radio and/or the ICS to relay patient information to the pilots or emergency department.

        External Syllabus Support. Clearance from area hospitals for landing at pads.

SAR-251   1.5   1 HH-46D/E

Goal. Introduce navigation procedures, distant area hospital
landing zones, and procedures for medical evacuation.

Requirement

(1) Brief/Discuss

    (a) Navigation procedures.

    (b) Area hospitals and their medical capabilities/locations.

    (c) Local medical protocols and flight surgeon recall
    procedures for hospital-to-hospital transfers.

    (d) Cabin preparation and rigging of the litters.

    (e) Use of radios in relaying patient information to the
    destination medical facility and use of the aircraft utility
    electrical power supply.

(2) Introduce/Demonstrate

    (a) Identify hospital Landing Zones.

    (b) Prepare the cabin to accept patients.

    (c) Assist SARMT with receiving the report from onscene
    providers, performing assessments and packaging patient for
    transport.

    (d) Assist SARMT in an actual/simulated medical evacuation to
    an airport/hospital facility while providing inflight
    care/monitoring.

    (e) Use aircraft electrical system and radio to contact
    receiving facility.

Performance Standard. SARRACUI shall safely prepare the cabin
for litter carriage using the stanchions, and assist the SMT with
enroute treatment of patients.

External Syllabus Support. Local EMS or hospital if desired.

SAR-252   1.5   1 HH-46D/E

Goal. Conduct day overland search patterns.

Requirement

(1) Brief/Discuss

    (a) Standard approach parameters and search patterns.

    (b) CAL procedures.

    (c) Standard ICS voice communications.

    (d) Remote hover coupler station.

(e) Emergency "Wave-Off" conditions and procedures.

(2) Introduce/Demonstrate

(a) Normal approach patterns and standard ICS terminology.

(b) Practice positioning the aircraft over a simulated survivor utilizing standard ICS terminology.

(c) Use remote hover coupler station for familiarization.

(d) Practice positioning the aircraft over a simulated survivor utilizing the remote hover station and standard ICS terminology.

Performance Standard. SARRACUI shall provide calls to the pilot to conduct a hover for crewmember deployment, maintaining within 2 meters of hover point.

SAR-253   1.5   R   1 HH-46D/E

Goal. Conduct day overland hoisting.

Requirement

(1) Brief/Discuss

(a) Hoist capability and limitations.

(b) Emergency procedures and troubleshooting techniques for hoist failure.

(c) Use of quick splice and Chicago grip.

(d) Review hand and arm signals and Aldis lamp signals.

(e) Rescue equipment functions, capacities, and limitations.

(f) Rigging of rescue equipment for hoisting evolutions.

(2) Introduce/Demonstrate

(a) Rigging of rescue strop, force penetrator/rescue seat, rescue litter, SAR litter, and rescue net.

(b) Perform a minimum of 2 hoisting evolutions, one with the rescue strop and one with the rescue net while acting as hoist operator.

(c) Demonstrate use of quick splice and Chicago grip.

(d) Perform a minimum of 2 hoisting evolutions with the Rescue litter and/or SAR litter while on the ground acting as the SARRAC.

Performance Standard. SARRAC shall rig and perform 2 hoisting evolutions as the hoist operator using the rescue strop and rescue net, and 2 hoisting evolutions from the ground as SARRAC using the Stokes litter and SAR litter.

SAR-254   1.5   R   1 HH-46D/E

Goal. Conduct day hoist operations with rescue devices utilizing the internal winch through the cabin floor rescue hatch and over the ramp.

Requirement

(1) Brief/Discuss

    (a) Internal winch capabilities and limitations.

    (b) Setup of rigging and use of winch control station and remote handgrip.

    (c) Emergency procedures and troubleshooting technique for winch failure.

    (d) Review standard ICS voice communications and hand and arm signals.

    (e) Review rigging of rescue equipment for hoisting evolutions.

(2) Introduce/Demonstrate

    (a) Setup of rigging and remote handgrip.

    (b) Complete a minimum of 2 hoisting evolutions with the rescue net and rescue litter while functioning as the winch operator.

    (c) Complete a minimum of 2 hoisting evolutions with the rescue seat and rescue/SAR litter while on the ground acting as the SARRAC.

Performance Standard. SARRACUI shall rig the remote handgrip and safely conduct 1 hoist as hoist operator and 3 hoists from the ground as SARRAC using the rescue net, Stokes litter, rescue seat, and SAR litter utilizing the internal winch and conducting the hoisting operations through the hellhole and over the ramp.

Prerequisite. SAR-253.

SAR-255   2.0   R   1 HH-46D/E

Goal. Conduct day overland SAREX.

Requirement

(1) Brief/Discuss

    (a) Overland SAR procedures, to include search patterns and CAL selection.

    (b) Crewmember responsibilities and cabin preparation.

    (c) Communication procedures.

(2) Introduce/Demonstrate

(a) Cabin preparation and actions while in route to scene.

(b) Conduct/assist in patient(s) assessment, treatment and packaging.

(c) Loading and securing patient(s) inside aircraft.

(d) Provide/assist in providing care while enroute to Medical Treatment Facility.

(e) Unloading and transferring patient(s).

(f) Familiarization with medical equipment on board.

Performance Standard. SARRACUI shall rig the remote handgrip and safely conduct hoists as hoist operator and from the ground as SARRAC using the rescue net, Stokes litter, rescue seat, and SAR litter.

Prerequisite. SAR-250/251, SAR-252, SAR-253.

External Syllabus Support. Local EMS/Fire Rescue if available.

SAR-256   1.5   R   1 HH-46D/E

Goal. Conduct day over water search and Doppler approaches.

Requirement

(1) Brief/Discuss

(a) Doppler/Coupler capabilities and procedures to include standard terminology and remote hover station.

(b) Crewmember responsibility during approach procedures.

(c) Flare capabilities, arming/disarming, and deployment techniques.

(d) Ordnance hazards and safety precautions.

(2) Introduce/Demonstrate

(a) Flare deployment.

(b) Voice communication using standard terminology.

(c) Verbal control of aircraft movements during a manual approach. SARRACUI will complete a minimum of 2 manual approach evolutions.

(d) Operation of the remote hover station during a coupled approach. SARRACUI will complete a minimum of 2 coupled approach evolutions.

Performance Standard. SARRACUI shall provide calls to the pilot to conduct a hover for crewmember deployment, maintaining within 2 meters of hover point. The SARRACUI will safely conduct simulated hoisting operations utilizing the Rescue Strop, Rescue Litter, SAR litter, and Rescue Net. SARRACUI will maintain a hover utilizing the crew chiefs Remote Hover Coupler Station, and maintain within 2 meters of hover point.

Ordnance. 1 Mk-25 Flare, 1 Mk-58 Flare.

SAR-258   1.5   R   1 HH-46D/E

Goal. Conduct day Rescue Swimmer deployment and recovery with rescue strop and net.

Requirements

(1) Brief/Discuss

    (a) Impact of sea state and weather concerning swimmer deployments.

    (b) Swimmer deployments and recovery procedures.

    (c) Survivor assessment, disentanglement, and recovery procedures.

    (d) Short haul purpose and procedures.

    (e) Normal and emergency hoisting procedures.

    (f) ICS communications and standard hand and arm signals.

    (g) Ordnance hazards and safety precautions.

(2) Introduce/Demonstrate

    (a) Day jump deployments.

    (b) Day single and dual hoist recovery utilizing the rescue strop with a simulated survivor.

    (c) Day single and dual hoist recovery utilizing the rescue net with a simulated survivor.

    (d) Short haul to simulated survivor.

Performance Standard. SARRAC shall safely conduct 3 day jumps from 10/10 or 15/0 and recover via rescue strop and rescue net. SARRAC shall safely perform a short haul on 1 of the recoveries.

Prerequisites. SAR-253, SAR-256.

Ordnance. 1 Mk-25 Flare, 1 Mk-58 Flare.

External Syllabus Support. Safety boat/aircraft with safety swimmer. Survivors as required.

SAR-259   1.5   R   1 HH-46D/E

Goal. Conduct day Rescue Swimmer deployment and recovery with the stokes and SAR litters.

Requirements

(1) <u>Brief/Discuss</u>

(a) Impact of sea state and weather concerning swimmer deployments.

(b) Swimmer deployments and recoveries.

(c) Survivor assessment, disentanglement, and recovery procedures.

(d) The use of the trail line assembly.

(e) Normal and emergency hoisting procedures.

(f) ICS communications and hand and arm signals.

(g) Ordnance hazards and safety precautions.

(2) <u>Introduce/Demonstrate</u>

(a) Perform a minimum of 2 day jump deployments and recoveries.

(b) Perform a minimum of 1 SAR litter deployment and recovery with a simulated survivor.

(c) Perform a minimum of 1 Rescue (Stokes) litter deployment and recovery with a simulated survivor.

<u>Performance Standard</u>. SARRAC shall safely conduct 2 day jumps from 10/10 or 15/0 and recover simulated survivor with Stokes litter and rescue litter.

<u>Prerequisites</u>. SAR-258.

<u>Ordnance</u>. 1 Mk-25 Flare, 1 Mk-58 Flare.

<u>External Syllabus Support</u>. Safety boat/aircraft with safety swimmer. Survivors as required.

<u>SAR-260</u>   <u>1.5</u>   <u>R</u>   <u>1 HH-46D/E</u>

<u>Goal</u>. Conduct day SAR boat hoist.

<u>Requirement</u>

(1) <u>Brief/Discuss</u>

(a) Normal and emergency procedures to include standard ICS terminology and hand and arm signals.

(b) Aircraft approach procedures and positioning.

(c) Special considerations when operating around a boat or ship to include the effects of sea state and obstacles.

(d) SARRAC/SMT and equipment hook-up procedures.

(2) <u>Demonstrate</u>

(a) Deployment and recovery of SARRAC/SARMT to the boat or ship.

(b) Hoisting procedures utilizing the rescue/SAR litter, rescue net, and rescue strop.

(c) Conduct a minimum of 2 rescue/SAR litter deployment and recoveries utilizing the trail line as SARRAC on deck.

(d) Conduct a minimum of 1 recovery utilizing the rescue strop.

<u>Performance Standard</u>. SARRAC shall conduct deployment from a hover to the deck of a boat or ship and conduct 2 deployment and recoveries of simulated survivor using Stokes and/or SAR litters and trail line, and 1 recovery via rescue strop.

<u>Prerequisites</u>. SAR-253, SAR-256, SAR-258.

<u>External Syllabus Support</u>. Safety boat that is suitable for hoisting from (i.e. US Coast Guard or affiliate, US military vessels, local municipal rescue/FD water rescue units, etc.) Safety swimmer and survivors as required.

332. <u>CORE SKILL ADVANCED TRAINING</u>

1. <u>Night Vision Goggles</u>

a. <u>Purpose</u>. Develop proficiency required to safely conduct basic operations, navigation, and search and rescue patterns utilizing NVGs.

b. <u>Prerequisite</u>. Completion of NVG Night Lab and the following flights shall be complete.

(1) FAM-200

(2) EP-201

(3) CAL-221

c. <u>Crew Requirements</u>. CCNSSI.

d. <u>Flight Training (4 Flights, 6.0 Hours)</u>

<u>NVG-300</u>   <u>1.5</u>   <u>R</u>   <u>1 HH-46D/E</u>   <u>NS</u>

<u>Goal</u>. NVG familiarization flight in HLL conditions.

<u>Requirement</u>

(1) <u>Brief/Discuss</u>

(a) Use and limitations of NVGs.

(b) NVG tube/battery failures and emergency procedures.

(c) Lookout doctrine and obstacle clearances.

(2) <u>Introduce/Demonstrate</u>. Wearing and use of NVGs.

<u>Performance Standard</u>. SARRACUI shall be able to safely perform familiarization maneuvers while on NVGs per NFM, and MAWTS-1 NVG Manual.

<u>NVG-301</u>   <u>1.5</u>   <u>R</u>   <u>1 HH-46D/E</u>   <u>NS</u>

<u>Goal</u>. Develop proficiency in confined area landings using NVGs. This flight may be conducted in HLL or LLL conditions.

<u>Requirement</u>

(1) <u>Brief/Discuss</u>

(a) Use and limitations of NVGs to include emergency procedures.

(b) Confined area landing approaches and aircraft clearances.

(c) Approach procedures.

(2) <u>Introduce/Demonstrate</u>. Wearing and use of NVGs while conducting a minimum of 3 CALs.

<u>Performance Standard</u>. SARRACUI shall be able to safely perform SAR operations while on NVGs per NFM, and MAWTS-1 NVG Manual.

<u>Prerequisite</u>. NVG-300.

<u>NVG-302</u>   <u>1.5</u>   <u>1 HH-46D/E</u>   <u>NS</u>

<u>Goal</u>. Develop proficiency with NVGs during night low level navigation. This flight may be conducted in HLL or LLL conditions.

<u>Requirement</u>

(1) <u>Brief/Discuss</u>

(a) Use and limitations of NVGs to include emergency procedures.

(b) Interior and exterior aircraft lighting.

(c) Hospital landing zones in the night environment.

(2) <u>Introduce/Demonstrate</u>. Wearing and use of NVGs while conducting navigation and search patterns.

<u>Performance Standard</u>. SARRACUI shall demonstrate ability to assist pilots and crewchief in search pattern, maintain good search doctrine, ensure effective CRM for navigation and obstacle clearance, and utilize proper terminology.

<u>Prerequisite</u>. NVG-300.

2. <u>Night Search and Rescue</u>

a. <u>Purpose</u>. Familiarize the SARRACUI with the SAR mission and operations, aircraft lighting systems and emergency procedures at night. To develop proficiency in loading cargo/passengers, in-flight procedures, SAR procedures and requirements, and knowledge of safety regulations.

b. <u>General</u>. The T&R Program Manual addresses the commanding officer's authority to modify this training as required. Personnel will complete the appropriate ground schools prior to beginning the flight-training syllabus. A SARRAC NATOPS instructor will monitor the SARRACUI's progress during the flight-training syllabus.

c. <u>Prerequisite</u>

(1) SARRAC's may begin the night SAR syllabus training prior to completion of the entire day SAR syllabus. Prior to commencement of a night SAR syllabus flight, the corresponding day SAR syllabus flight shall be completed.

(2) The NVG syllabus must be complete.

d. <u>Crew Requirements</u>. SARRACI/SARRACUI.

e. <u>Flight Training (8 Flights, 13.0 Hours)</u>

<u>NSAR-320</u>   1.5   1 HH-46D/E   <u>N</u>

   <u>Goal</u>. Conduct night overland search patterns.

   <u>Requirement</u>

   (1) <u>Brief/Discuss</u>

       (a) Aircraft Lighting Systems.

       (b) Standard approach parameters and search patterns.

       (c) CAL procedures.

       (d) Standard ICS voice communications.

       (e) Remote hover coupler station.

       (f) Emergency "Wave-Off" conditions and procedures.

   (2) <u>Introduce/Demonstrate</u>

       (a) Normal approach patterns and standard ICS terminology.

       (b) Perform a minimum of 3 CALS. One should be conducted while acting in the capacity of the crew chief.

       (c) Practice positioning the aircraft over a simulated survivor utilizing standard ICS terminology.

       (d) Use remote hover coupler station for familiarization.

(e) Practice positioning the aircraft over a simulated survivor utilizing the remote hover station and standard ICS terminology.

Performance Standard. SARRACUI shall provide calls to the pilot to conduct a hover for crewmember deployment, maintaining within 2 meters of hover point.

Prerequisite. SAR-252.

NSAR-321   1.5   R   1 HH-46D/E   N

Goal. Conduct night overland hoisting operations.

Requirement

(1) Brief/Discuss

   (a) Hoist capability and limitations.

   (b) Emergency procedures and troubleshooting techniques for hoist failure.

   (c) Review hand and arm signals and Aldis lamp signals.

   (d) Rigging and chemlite placement for rescue equipment for hoisting evolutions.

(2) Introduce/Demonstrate

   (a) Rigging of chemlites on the rescue strop, force penetrator/rescue seat, rescue litter, SAR litter, and rescue net.

   (b) Perform a minimum of 2 hoisting evolutions, 1 with the rescue strop and 1 with the rescue net while acting as hoist operator.

   (c) Perform a minimum of 2 hoisting evolutions with the Rescue litter and/or SAR litter while on the ground acting as the SARRAC.

Performance Standard. SARRAC shall rig and perform 2 hoisting evolutions as the hoist operator using the rescue strop and rescue net, and 2 hoisting evolutions from the ground as SARRAC using the Stokes litter and SAR litter.

Prerequisite. NSAR-321, SAR-203.

NSAR-322   2.0   R   1 HH-46D/E   N

Goal. Conduct night overland SAR exercise.

Requirement

(1) Brief/Discuss

   (a) Overland SAR procedures, to include search patterns and CAL selection.

(b) Crewmember responsibilities and cabin preparation.

(c) Communication procedures.

(2) Introduce/Demonstrate

(a) Cabin preparation and actions while enroute to scene.

(b) Assist SMT in patient(s) assessment, treatment and packaging.

(c) Loading and securing patient(s) inside aircraft.

(d) Assist SMT in providing care while enroute to Medical Treatment Facility.

(e) Unloading and transferring patient(s).

Performance Standard. SARRACUI shall demonstrate proficiency in patient assessments and providing patient care.

Prerequisite. SAR-255, NSAR-320, NSAR-321.

External Syllabus Support. Local EMS/Fire Rescue if available.

NSAR-323   1.5   1 HH-46D/E   N

Goal. Conduct night over water SAR approach training.
Requirement

(1) Brief/Discuss

(a) Doppler/Coupler capabilities and procedures to include standard terminology and remote hover station.

(b) Crewmember responsibility during approach procedures.

(c) Flare capabilities, arming/disarming, and deployment techniques.

(d) Ordnance hazards and safety precautions.

(2) Introduce/Demonstrate

(a) Flare deployment.

(b) Voice communication using standard terminology.

(c) Verbal control of aircraft movements during a manual approach. SARRACUI will complete a minimum of 2 manual approach evolutions.

(d) Operation of the remote hover station during a coupled approach. SARRACUI will complete a minimum of 2 coupled approach evolutions.

Performance Standard. SARRACUI shall provide calls to the pilot to conduct a hover for crewmember deployment, maintaining within 2 meters of hover point. The SARRACUI will safely conduct simulated hoisting operations utilizing the Rescue Strop, Rescue

Litter, SAR litter, and Rescue Net. SARRACUI will maintain a hover utilizing the crew chief's Remote Hover Coupler Station, and maintain within 2 meters of hover point.

Prerequisite. NSAR-256.

Ordnance. 1 Mk-25, 1 Mk-58 Flare.

NSAR-330   1.5   R   1 HH-46D/E   N

Goal. Conduct night Rescue Swimmer deployments and recoveries (Night Water Works) utilizing the rescue strop and rescue net.

Requirements

(1) Brief/Discuss

    (a) Impact of sea state and weather concerning swimmer deployments in the night environment.

    (b) Swimmer deployments and recoveries procedures.

    (c) Survivor assessment, disentanglement, and recovery procedures.

    (d) Normal and emergency hoisting procedures.

    (e) ICS communications and standard hand and arm signals.

    (f) Ordnance hazards and safety precautions.

(2) Introduce/Demonstrate

    (a) Night deployment (via hoist) and dual hoist recovery utilizing the rescue strop with a simulated survivor.

    (b) Night deployment (via hoist) and dual hoist recovery utilizing the rescue net with a simulated survivor.

Performance Standard. SARRAC shall safely conduct 2 night deployments from 50 foot hover via hoist and recover via rescue strop and rescue net.

Prerequisites. SAR-258, NSAR-320, NSAR-321, NSAR-323.

Ordnance. 1 Mk-25 Flare, 1 Mk-58 Flare.

External Syllabus Support. Safety boat/aircraft with safety swimmer. Survivors as required.

NSAR-331   1.5   R   1 HH-46D/E   N

Goal. Conduct night Rescue Swimmer deployments and recoveries utilizing the stokes and SAR litters.

Requirements

(1) Brief/Discuss

   (a) Impact of sea state and weather concerning swimmer deployments.

   (b) Swimmer deployments and recoveries.

   (c) Survivor assessment, disentanglement, and recovery procedures.

   (d) The use of the trail line assembly.

   (e) Normal and emergency hoisting procedures.

   (f) ICS communications and hand and arm signals.

   (g) Ordnance hazards and safety precautions.

(2) Introduce/Demonstrate

   (a) Perform a minimum of 1 SAR litter deployment and recovery with a simulated survivor.

   (b) Perform a minimum of 1 Rescue (Stokes) litter deployment and recovery with a simulated survivor.

Performance Standard. SARRACUI shall safely conduct 2 night deployments from 50 foot hover and recover simulated survivor with Stokes litter and rescue litter.

Prerequisites. SAR-258, NSAR-320, NSAR-321, NSAR-323.

Ordnance. 1 Mk-25 Flare, 1 Mk-58 Flare.

External Syllabus Support. Safety boat/aircraft with safety swimmer. Survivors as required.

NSAR-332   1.5   R   1 HH-46D/E   N

Goal. Conduct night SAR boat hoist training.

Requirement

(1) Brief/Discuss

   (a) Normal and emergency procedures to include standard ICS terminology and hand and arm signals.

   (b) Aircraft approach procedures and positioning.

   (c) Special considerations when operating around a boat or ship to include the effects of sea state and obstacles.

   (d) SARRAC/SMT and equipment hook-up procedures.

(2) <u>Introduce/Demonstrate</u>

(a) Deployment and recovery of SARRAC/SMT to the boat or ship.

(b) Hoisting procedures utilizing the rescue/SAR litter, rescue net, and rescue strop.

(c) Conduct a minimum of 2 rescue/SAR litter deployment and recoveries utilizing the trail line as SARRAC on deck.
(d) Conduct a minimum of 1 recovery utilizing the rescue strop.

<u>Performance Standard</u>. SARRAC shall conduct deployment from a hover to the deck of a boat or ship and conduct 2 deployment and recoveries of simulated survivor using Stokes and SAR litters and trail line, and one recovery via rescue strop.

<u>Prerequisites</u>. SAR-260, NSAR-330.

<u>External Syllabus Support</u>. Safety boat with safety swimmer that is suitable for hoisting from (i.e. US Coast Guard or affiliate, US military vessels, local municipal rescue/FD water rescue units, etc.) Survivors as required.

<u>NSAR-333</u>   <u>1.5</u>   <u>R</u>   <u>1 HH-46D/E</u>   <u>N</u>

<u>Goal</u>. Practice night SAR boat hoist training.

<u>Requirement</u>

(1) <u>Brief/Discuss</u>

(a) Normal and emergency procedures to include standard ICS terminology and hand and arm signals.

(b) Aircraft approach procedures and positioning.

(c) Special considerations when operating around a boat or ship to include the effects of sea state and obstacles.

(d) SARRAC/SMT and equipment hook-up procedures.

(2) <u>Practice</u>

(a) Deployment and recovery of SARRAC/SMT to the boat or ship.

(b) Hoisting procedures utilizing the rescue/SAR litter, rescue net, and rescue strop.

(c) Conduct a minimum of 2 rescue/SAR litter deployment and recoveries utilizing the trail line as SARRAC on deck.

(d) Conduct a minimum of 1 recovery utilizing the rescue strop.

<u>Performance Standard</u>. SARRAC shall conduct deployment from a hover to the deck of a boat or ship and conduct 2 deployment and

recoveries of simulated survivor using Stokes and SAR litters and trail line, and one recovery via rescue strop.

Prerequisites. SAR-260, NSAR-330.

External Syllabus Support. Safety boat with safety swimmer that is suitable for hoisting from (i.e. US Coast Guard or affiliate, US military vessels, local municipal rescue/FD water rescue units, etc.) Survivors as required.

NSAR-340   2.0   R   1 HH-46D/E   N

Goal. Participate in a night over water SAREX (SAR Swimmer only).

Requirement

(1) Brief/Discuss

    (a) Over water SAR procedures.

    (b) Search Patterns.

    (c) Night/low visibility procedures.

    (d) Medical treatment procedures/protocols.

    (e) Transportation protocols.

    (f) Ordnance hazards and safety precautions.

(2) Introduce/Demonstrate

    (a) Conduct swimmer deployment to a simulated rescue scenario involving multiple survivors with various injuries. Maintain high situational awareness and demonstrate proper SARRAC procedures.

    (b) Demonstrate proper rescue techniques and conduct/assist in medical treatment of injured patients.

Performance Standard. SARRACUI shall rig the remote handgrip and safely conduct hoists as hoist operator and from the ground or water as SARRAC using the rescue net, Stokes litter, rescue seat, and SAR litter.

Prerequisites. SAR-255, NSAR-320 through NSAR-332.

Ordnance. 1 MK-25 Flare, 1 MK-58 Flare.

External Syllabus Support. Local EMS/Fire Rescue if required. Safety boat with safety swimmer that is suitable for hoisting from (i.e. US Coast Guard or affiliate, US military vessels, local municipal rescue/FD water rescue units, etc.) Survivors as required.

NSAR-341   2.0   R   1 HH-46D/E   N

Goal. Participate in a night over land SAREX (Med Tech only).

Requirement

(1) Brief/Discuss

(a) Over land SAR procedures.

(b) Search Patterns.

(c) Night/low visibility procedures.

(d) Medical treatment procedures/protocols.

(e) Transportation protocols.

(f) Ordnance hazards and safety precautions.

(2) Introduce/Demonstrate

(a) Conduct night swimmer deployment to a simulated rescue scenario involving multiple survivors with various injuries. Maintain good situational awareness and demonstrate proper SARRAC procedures.

(b) Demonstrate proper rescue techniques and conduct/assist in medical treatment of injured patients.

Performance Standard. SARRACUI shall rig the remote handgrip and safely conduct hoists as hoist operator and from the ground or water as SARRAC using the rescue net, Stokes litter, rescue seat, and SAR litter.

Prerequisites. SAR-255, NSAR-320 through NSAR-332.

External Syllabus Support. Local EMS/Fire Rescue if required. Safety boat with safety swimmer that is suitable for hoisting from (i.e. US Coast Guard or affiliate, US military vessels, local municipal rescue/FD water rescue units, etc.) Survivors as required.

333. CORE PLUS TRAINING

1. Helicopter Inland Rescue Aircrewman (HIRA) Rappel Operations

a. Purpose. Develop the SARRACs knowledge and proficiency of rappel procedures, equipment limitations, equipment set-up and usage, and safety checks.

b. General

(1) SARRAC must have completed Helicopter Rappel Training Ground School (HSC-3) as required by OPNAVINST 3130.6 (series).

(2) Prior to beginning flight training, SARRAC shall complete a local rappel ground-training syllabus and meet all requirements as indicated in applicable SAR related publications.

(3) All rappel-training evolutions shall be conducted with the use of the belay line for "Bagless" rappels or a HIRA qualified safety observer tending the free end of the rappel rope during a "Standard" rappel.

(4) Only HIRA qualified personnel shall act as a survivor for all training short haul evolutions.

(5) Rappel and hoisting operations should not be conducted while using NVGs.

(6) Upon completion of this stage of training, SARRAC should be able to correctly perform all required equipment set-ups and safely rappel from the helicopter.

    c. Crew Requirements. HIRAI/HIRAUT.

    d. Flight Training (4 flights, 6 hours)

RAP-400   1.5   1 HH-46D/E

    Goal. Introduce SAR rappelling operations.

    Requirement

    (1) Brief/Discuss

        (a) Safety considerations.

        (b) Crew coordination and communication during rappel operations to include standard ICS terminology and hand and arm signals.

        (c) Equipment inventory, preflight inspection and set-up.

    (2) Introduce/Demonstrate

        (a) Rappel rope and belay line rigging and setups.

        (b) Conduct a minimum of 3 rappel descents, 2 standard rappels and 1 bagless rappel.

        (c) Demonstrate the 3 "Lock-off" techniques.

    Performance Standard. The SARRACUI should properly setup the rappel and belay line and conduct safety checks and conduct 3 rappel descents.

RAP-401   1.5   1 HH-46D/E

    Goal. Conduct SAR rappelling operations and introduce short haul Procedures.

    Requirement

    (1) Brief/Discuss

        (a) Safety considerations.

        (b) Crew coordination and communication during rappel operations to include standard ICS terminology and hand and arm signals.

          (c) Equipment inventory, preflight inspection and set-up.

          (d) Short haul procedures and lock-off techniques.

          (e) Hoisting Vest.

    (2) <u>Introduce/Demonstrate</u>

          (a) Rappel rope and belay line rigging and setups.

          (b) Short haul procedures and use of hoisting vest.

          (c) Conduct a minimum of 3 rappel descents with 1 ending and a short haul of a survivor in the hoisting vest.

<u>Performance Standard</u>. The SARRACUI should properly setup the rappel and belay line and conduct safety checks. The SARRACUI should perform 3 rappel descents and 1 short haul operation.

<u>Prerequisite</u>. RAP-400.

<u>RAP-402</u>   <u>1.5</u>   <u>R</u>   <u>1 HH-46D/E</u>

<u>Goal</u>. Conduct SAR rappelling and short haul operations.

<u>Requirement</u>

    (1) <u>Brief/Discuss</u>

          (a) Safety considerations.

          (b) Crew coordination and communication during rappel operations to include standard ICS terminology and hand and arm signals.

          (c) Equipment inventory, preflight inspection and set-up.

          (d) Short haul procedures and lock-off techniques.

          (e) Rappelling with equipment and short haul procedures with the rescue litter.

    (2) <u>Introduce/Demonstrate</u>

          (a) Rappel rope and belay line rigging and setups.

          (b) Conduct a minimum of 3 rappel descents with equipment.

          (c) Two descents should end with the short haul of a simulated survivor in the rescue litter.

<u>Performance Standard</u>. The SARRACUI should properly setup the rappel and belay line and conduct safety checks. The SARRACUI should perform 3 rappel descents and 1 short haul operation of a simulated survivor in the Stokes litter.

<u>Prerequisite</u>. RAP-401.

RAP-403   1.5   R   1 HH-46D/E

Goal. Conduct HIRA Evaluation.

Requirement

(1) Brief/Discuss

(a) Safety considerations.

(b) Crew coordination and communication during rappel operations to include standard ICS terminology and hand and arm signals.

(c) Equipment inventory, preflight inspection and set-up.

(d) Short haul procedures and lock-off techniques.

(2) Introduce/Demonstrate

(a) Rappel rope and belay line rigging and setups.

(b) Standard and bag-less rappels with equipment.

(c) Conduct a minimum of 2 rappel descents with each ending with a short haul of a simulated survivor in the rescue litter.

Performance Standard. The SARRACUI should properly setup the rappel and belay line and conduct safety checks without assistance. The SARRACUI should perform 2 rappel descents ending in short haul operations of a simulated survivor in the Stokes litter.

Prerequisite. RAP-402.

340. INSTRUCTOR UNDER TRAINING (SAR NATOPS)

1. Purpose. Standardize the procedures qualifying syllabus instructors within individual units.

2. General

a. The SARRACIUT must demonstrate proficiency in instructing all evolutions in this stage.

b. Upon completion of this stage the SARRACIUT shall be designated a SAR Rescue Aircrewman Instructor (SARRACI).

c. Crew Requirements. SARRACI/SARRACIUT.

d. Prerequisites. Core Skill Advanced Stage complete.

e. Flight Training (4 Flights, 7.5 Hours)

IUT-500   1.5   E   1 HH-46D/E

Goal. Demonstrate instructional techniques during day
FAM/CAL/INT maneuvers and procedures.

Requirement

(1) Brief/Discuss

   (a) Instructional Techniques.

   (b) Crew responsibilities during start-up, taxi, take-off,
   in-flight emergencies, and landings.

   (c) Crew responsibilities and communications during SAR
   procedures.

(2) Introduce/Demonstrate. Thorough knowledge of all procedures
related to Familiarization, CALs, and Internal sorties.

Performance Standard. SARRACIUT shall demonstrate the ability to
instruct familiarization maneuvers and internal patient, cargo
and passenger embarking and debarking. SARRACIUT shall
demonstrate instructional techniques during flight.

IUT-501   1.5   E   1 HH-46D/E

Goal. Demonstrate instructional techniques during Land SAR
Exercise.

Requirement

(1) Brief/Discuss

   (a) Instructional Techniques.

   (b) SARRAC responsibilities for planning land SAREX.

   (c) Evaluation guidelines and standards as identified by SOP.

   (d) Crew responsibilities and communications during land
   SAREX.

(2) Introduce/Demonstrate. Thorough knowledge of all procedures
related to planning and evaluating a land SAREX.

Performance Standard. SARRACIUT shall demonstrate the ability to
instruct SAR maneuvers, including demonstrating and introducing
search patterns and techniques, and hover and recovery maneuvers
to SARRACs under instruction.

Prerequisite. IUT-500.

IUT-502   1.5   E   1 HH-46D/E

Goal. Demonstrate instructional techniques during over water SAR
operations.

Requirement

(1) Brief/Discuss

    (a) Instructional Techniques.

    (b) SARRAC responsibilities while in route to training site.

    (c) Crew responsibilities and communications during overwater SAR operations.

(2) Introduce/Demonstrate. Thorough knowledge of all procedures related to planning and assisting with an over water SAR exercises.

Performance Standard. SARRACIUT shall demonstrate the ability to instruct SAR maneuvers, including demonstrating and introducing over water search patterns and techniques, and hover and recovery maneuvers to SARRACs under instruction.

Prerequisite. IUT-501.

Ordnance. 1 MK-25, 1 MK-58.

External Syllabus Support. Safety boat with safety swimmer that is suitable for hoisting from (i.e. US Coast Guard or affiliate, US military vessels, local municipal rescue/FD water rescue units, etc.) Survivors as required.

IUT-503   1.5   E   1 HH-46D/E

Goal. Demonstrate instructional techniques during water bucket operations (Bambi Buckets).

Requirement

(1) Brief/Discuss

    (a) Crew coordination.

    (b) SARRAC responsibilities during water bucket operations.

    (c) Emergency procedures.

(2) Review

    (a) Water bucket operations.

    (b) Pre-flight and pos-flight procedures and requirements for water bucket operations.

Performance Standard. SARRAC shall demonstrate the ability to instruct water bucket operations to include proper rigging, deployment and post flight care of water bucket.

IUT-504   3.0   E   1 HH-46D/E   (N)

Goal. Review all instructional techniques for SAR in flight procedures. This flight may be flown in a day or night environment.

Requirement

(1) Brief/Discuss

(a) Training site set-up and roles of simulated survivors to pertinent aircrew members.

(b) Special requests to simulate aircraft emergencies, failed gear, etc.

(c) Crew responsibilities and communications during SAR procedures.

(2) Introduce/Demonstrate. Thorough knowledge of all procedures related to planning and supervising an overwater SARRAC NATOPS Evaluation.

Performance Standard. SARRACIUT shall plan, coordinate, and conduct a SAREX unassisted.

Prerequisite. IUT-500, IUT-501, IUT-502, IUT-503.

Ordnance. 1 MK-25, 1 MK-58.

External Syllabus Support. Safety boat with safety swimmer that is suitable for hoisting from (i.e. US Coast Guard or affiliate, US military vessels, local municipal rescue/FD water rescue units, etc.) Survivors as required.

Additional Comments. Completion of the IUT-503 flight will satisfy the annual NATOPS Evaluation requirement.

341. INSTRUCTOR UNDER TRAINING: GRADUATE LEVEL COURSES (NSSI). Not applicable. NVD instruction is provided by the SAR Crew Chief NSSI.

350. REQUIREMENTS, QUALIFICATIONS AND DESIGNATIONS

1. Purpose. To qualify the SARRACUI for designation as a SARRAC/HIRA or to complete the annual NATOPS evaluation.

2. Prerequisite

a. Completion of all required flights as specified by the individual's training syllabus.

b. Minimum of 50 flight hours for initial SARRAC.

3. Crew Requirements. SARRACI/SARRACUI.

4. Flight Training (3 Flights, 6.0 Hours)

RQD-600   1.5   E   1 HH-46D/E   (N)

Goal. Annual NATOPS Evaluation.

Requirement. Perform a flight per the HH-46 NATOPS Flight Manual.

Performance Standard. The performance expected by the evaluator in this flight shall be commensurate with the experience level of the SARRAC under evaluation.

RQD-602   3.0   E   1 HH-46D/E   (N)

Goal. SARRAC/HIRA qualification evaluation.

Requirement. A SARRAC/HIRA instructor will grade the SARRACUI's performance per the NATOPS Flight Manual, OPNAVINST 3130.6 and applicable SAR and medical publications.

Performance Standard. The performance expected by the evaluator in this flight shall be commensurate with the experience level of the SARRAC under evaluation.

Ordnance. 1 MK-25, 1 MK-58.

External Syllabus Support. Safety boat with safety swimmer that is suitable for hoisting from (i.e. US Coast Guard or affiliate, US military vessels, local municipal rescue/FD water rescue units, etc.) Survivors as required.

RQD-640   1.5   R, E   1 HH-46D/E

Goal. Crew Resource Management (CRM) Evaluation.

Requirement. A SARRAC/HIRA instructor will evaluate the SARRACUI's knowledge and application of CRM during brief, flight, and debrief. This flight is to be flown in accordance with the current edition of OPNAVINST 1542.7 and may be flown with any other syllabus flight.

Performance Standard. SARRAC shall demonstrate effective use of the 7 CRM critical skill areas.

360. EXPENDABLE ORDNANCE REQUIREMENTS. These requirements are based on a "per crew" basis per OPNAVNOTE 8010.

ORDNANCE	200 SERIES	300 SERIES	500 SERIES	600 SERIES	ANNUAL*
Mk-25 Flares	3	4	2	1	10
Mk-58 Flares	3	4	2	1	10

* Annual Ordnance requirements maintain an aircrew member at 85% MRP per T&R Program Manual.

361. SYLLABUS MATRICES. These matrices display specific event information such as; flight/simulator hours, refly interval, prerequisites, CRP, chaining, etc.

									HH-46D/E SAR SARRAC				
									CORE SKILL BASIC (200 SERIES)				
STAGE	TRNG CODE	FLT HOURS	SIM HOURS	REFLY INTERVAL	POI	EVAL	TOTAL A/C	TYPE	CONDITIONS	PREQ	EVENT DESC	CRP	CHAINING	EVENT CONV
									FAM / EP				
FAM	200	1.5		*			1	A			AREA FAM	1.0		108
EP	201	1.5		*	R		1	A			EP FAM	0.5		109
		3.0	0.0									1.5		
									CAL				
CAL	220	1.5		*			1	A			INTRO DAY CAL	0.5		120
CAL	221	1.5		*	R		1	A		220	REV DAY CAL	0.5		
		3.0	0.0									1.0		
									INT				
INT	230	1.5		*	R		1	A			"E" - INT CARGO	1.0		130
INT	231	1.5		*	R		1	A		230	"D" - INT CARGO	1.0		131
		3.0	0.0									2.0		
									FF				
FF	240	1.5		*	R		1	A			BAMBI BUCKET	0.5		140
		1.5	0.0									0.5		
									SAR				
SAR	250	1.5		365			1	A		200,201,221, 230,231	LOCAL HOSP LZ	1.0		200
SAR	251	1.5		365			1	A		200,201,221, 230,231	DISTANT HOSP LZ	1.0		201
SAR	252	1.5		365			1	A		200,201,221, 230,231	DAY SEARCH	1.0		202
SAR	253	1.5		365	R		1	A		200,201,221, 230,231	DAY HOISTING	1.0		203
SAR	254	1.5		365	R		1	A		253	DAY RAMP HOISTING	1.0		204
SAR	255	2.0		365	R		1	A		250,251,252, 253	DAY SAREX	1.0	253,252, 251,250, 220	205
SAR	256	1.5		365	R		1	A			DAY DOPPLER	1.0		206
SAR	258	1.5		365	R		1	A		253,256	DAY SAR SWIM (STROP)	1.0 0	256	207
SAR	259	1.5		365	R		1	A		258	DAY SAR SWIM (LITTER)	1.0 0	256	208
SAR	260	1.5		365	R		1	A		253,256,258	DAY BOAT HOIST	1.0 0	259,258, 256	209
		15.5	0.0									10.		
									PHASE TOTAL				
FLT HRS		26.0	0.0	SIM HRS								15	CRP TOTAL	

										HH-46D/E SAR SARRAC				
									CORE SKILL ADVANCED (300 SERIES)					
STAGE	TRNG CODE	FLT HOURS	SIM HOURS	REFLY INTERVAL	POI	EVAL	TOTAL A/C	TYPE	CONDITIONS	PREQ	EVENT DESC	CRP	CHAINING	EVENT CONV
							NVG							
NVG	300	1.5		365	R		1	A	NS	200,201, 221	NVG HLL FAM	1.5		300
NVG	301	1.5		365	R		1	A	NS	300	NVG CAL	1.5	300	301
NVG	302	1.5		365			1	A	NS	300	NVG NAV	1.5	301,300	
		4.5	0									4.5		
							NSAR							
NSAR	320	1.5		365			1	A	N	252	NIGHT SAR PATTERNS	1.5	302,301,300,252	321
NSAR	321	1.5		365	R		1	A	N	321,203	NIGHT SAR HOIST	1.5	302,301,300,253	322
NSAR	322	2.0		365	R		1	A	N	255,320, 321	NIGHT SAREX	2.0	321,320,302,301,300, 255,253,252,251,250, 220	323
NSAR	323	1.5		365			1	A	N	256	NIGHT WATER APP	1.5	302,300,256	324
NSAR	330	1.5		365	R		1	A	N	258,320, 321,323	NIGHT WATER WORKS	1.5	323,302,300,258,256	325
NSAR	331	1.5		365	R		1	A	N	258,320, 321,323	NIGHT SWIM (STOKES)	1.5	323,302,300,259,256	326
NSAR	332	1.5		365	R		1	A	N	260,330	NIGHT BOAT HOIST	1.5	331,302,300,260,259	327
NSAR	333	1.5		365	R		1	A	N	260,330	REV NIGHT BOAT HOIST	1.5	332,331,302,300,260, 259	328
NSAR	340	2.0		365	R		1	A	N	255,320, 321,322, 323,330, 331,332	NIGHT SAREX (SWIMMER)	1.5	331,330,323,302,300, 256	
NSAR	341	2.0		365	R		1	A	N	255,320, 321,322, 323,330, 331,332	NIGHT SAREX (MED TECH)	1.5	322,321,320,302,301, 300,255,253,252,251, 250,220	
		16.5	0									15.5		
							PHASE TOTAL							
FLT HRS		21.0	0	SIM HRS								20.0	CRP TOTAL	

CORE PLUS (400 SERIES)

STAGE	TRNG CODE	FLT HOURS	SIM HOURS	REFLY INTERVAL	POI	EVAL	TOTAL A/C	TYPE	CONDITIONS	PREQ	EVENT DESC	CRP	CHAINING	EVENT CONV
											RAP			
RAP	400	1.5		365			1	A			SAR RAPPEL	1.0		400
RAP	401	1.5		365			1	A		400	SHORT HAUL	1.0	400	401
RAP	402	1.5		365	R		1	A		401	RAPPEL & SHORT HAUL	1.5	401,400	402
RAP	403	1.5		365	R		1	A		402	HIRA EVAL	1.5	402,401,400	403
		6.0		0.0								5.0		
							PHASE TOTAL							
FLT HRS		6.0		0.0	SIM HRS					5.0	CRP TOTAL			

HH-46D/E SAR SARRAC

INSTRUCTOR TRAINING (500 SERIES)

STAGE	TRNG CODE	FLT HOURS	SIM HOURS	REFLY INTERVAL	POI	EVAL	TOTAL A/C	TYPE	CONDITIONS	PREQ	EVENT DESC	CRP	CHAINING	EVENT CONV
											IUT			
IUT	500	1.5		*		X	1	A			IUT FAM	0.00		500
IUT	501	1.5		*		X	1	A		500	IUT LAND SAREX	0.00		501
IUT	502	1.5		*		X	1	A		501	IUT WATER SAREX	0.00		502
IUT	503	1.5		*		X	1	A			IUT BAMBI BUCKET	0.00		
IUT	504	3.0		*		X	1	A	(N)	500,501,502,503	IUT SAREX EVAL	0.00		503
		9.0	0.0									0.00		
							PHASE TOTAL							
FLT HRS		9.0	0.0	SIM HRS								0.00	CRP TOTAL	

REQUIREMENTS, QUALIFICATIONS, & DESIGNATIONS [RQD] (600 SERIES)

STAGE	TRNG CODE	FLT HOURS	SIM HOURS	REFLY INTERVAL	POI	EVAL	TOTAL A/C	TYPE	CONDITIONS	PREQ	EVENT DESC	CRP	CHAINING	EVENT CONV
											RQD			
RQD	600	1.5		365		X	1	A	(N)		NATOPS EVAL	0.00		600
RQD	602	3.0		365		X	1	A	(N)		SARRAC/HIRA EVAL	0.00		602
RQD	640	1.5		365		X	1	A	(N)		CRM	0.00		640
		6.0	0.0									0.00		
							PHASE TOTAL							
FLT HRS		6.0	0.0	SIM HRS								0.00	CRP TOTAL	

SYLLABUS EVENT CONVERSION MATRIX

OLD STAGE	OLD TRNG CODE	NEW STAGE	NEW TRNG CODE
		100 LEVEL	
FAM	108	FAM	200
	109	EP	201
CAL	120	CAL	220
INT	130	INT	230
	131		231
FF	140	FF	240

OLD STAGE	OLD TRNG CODE	NEW STAGE	NEW TRNG CODE
		200 LEVEL	
SAR	200	SAR	250
	201		251
	202		252
	203		253
	204		254
	205		255
	206		256
	207		258
	208		259
	209		260

OLD STAGE	OLD TRNG CODE	NEW STAGE	NEW TRNG CODE
		300 LEVEL	
NVG	300	NVG	300
	301		301
			302
	303		
NSAR	321		320
	322		321
	323		322
	324		323
	325		325
	326		326
	327		327
	328		328
			329

Figure 3-1.--SARRAC Syllabus Conversion Matrix.

SYLLABUS EVENT CONVERSION MATRIX

OLD STAGE	OLD TRNG CODE	NEW STAGE	NEW TRNG CODE
	400 LEVEL		
RAP	400	RAP	400
	401		401
	402		402
	403		403
FCLP	410		
	411		

OLD STAGE	OLD TRNG CODE	NEW STAGE	NEW TRNG CODE
	500 LEVEL		
IUT	500	IUT	500
	501		501
	502		502
			503
	503		504

OLD STAGE	OLD TRNG CODE	NEW STAGE	NEW TRNG CODE
	600 LEVEL		
RQD	600	RQD	600
	602		602
	640		640

Figure 3-1.--SARRAC Syllabus Conversion Matrix—Continued.